I0815574

AN ENGLISH VISION

FOREWORD BY THE EARL OF MORAY · PHOTOGRAPHY BY BEN PENTREATH
AN ENGLISH
Traditional Architecture and Decoration for Today

Ben Pentreath

VISION

RIZZOLI
NEW YORK
New York Paris London Milan

For Charlie and the dogs, Mavis, Sybil and Enid

A Note on Photography When I first embarked on this book, I realised that I needed to think in a slightly unconventional way about how I would organise the photography. After a few false starts, I understood that the only realistic way to achieve the images I was after was to take them myself.

Jan Baldwin, the brilliant photographer who shot my first two books, kindly gave me the name of her colleague Peter Dixon. Peter slowly taught me how to use a camera. I still have no idea what I am really doing, in the same way that I don't actually know what's happening when I drive a car. I press this pedal and it goes faster, and that pedal and it stops. It's rather the same with the camera. I have learnt to use the lenses and monitor the depth of vision, and I think I've always enjoyed composing photographs. But a detailed technical understanding will elude me forever. Thankfully, Peter is there to make magic out of my raw images.

On the early shoots, Peter was with me every step of the way. Very slowly, by watching what he was up to, I learnt these basic technical skills, and for much of the last year, if not longer, I've done the shoots for many of the houses and all of the buildings on my own. I've realised that, particularly when it comes to interiors photography, I no longer attempt to move anything. It's a lot easier to move the camera than to rearrange furniture to get the right shot. Necessity has dictated this approach, but I am very much enjoying shooting rooms as I find them.

Peter then carefully and skilfully processes the images. It has been a time-consuming task and hard, in a sense, for someone who hasn't seen the rooms or buildings in person to get the atmosphere right. I think he does so, unfailingly, every time. It has been an immensely collaborative effort, but it's still nice to say I have taken almost every photograph in this book. Everything has been shot with a Canon 5D Mark IV.

Page 1 A design for a new house in Guiting Power, Gloucestershire, 2020. For this notable west-facing site, I was inspired by the Arts and Crafts Movement and, in particular, by Edwin Lutyens's Little Thakeham, which he called 'the best of the bunch'. This design did not achieve planning approval.

Pages 2–3 The topiary garden at a house in Oxfordshire (see also pages 156–73). The brick and clay tile west wing of the house, peeping through the yew, was completed in 2015. White alliums look like mysterious giant dandelions in the dawn light.

These pages In the studio there is a collection of models that I have commissioned of unbuilt projects. On the left is a new house in Cheshire and, behind that, a temple folly in Dorset, made by Mulvaney & Rogers. In the left foreground is a Doric column group and in the right foreground a new house in Cambridgeshire, both made in cork by Dieter Collen. In the centre is my 2023 Driehaus Award, and in the right background is a large nineteenth-century architect's model of a Greek Doric portico, bought from Edward Hurst.

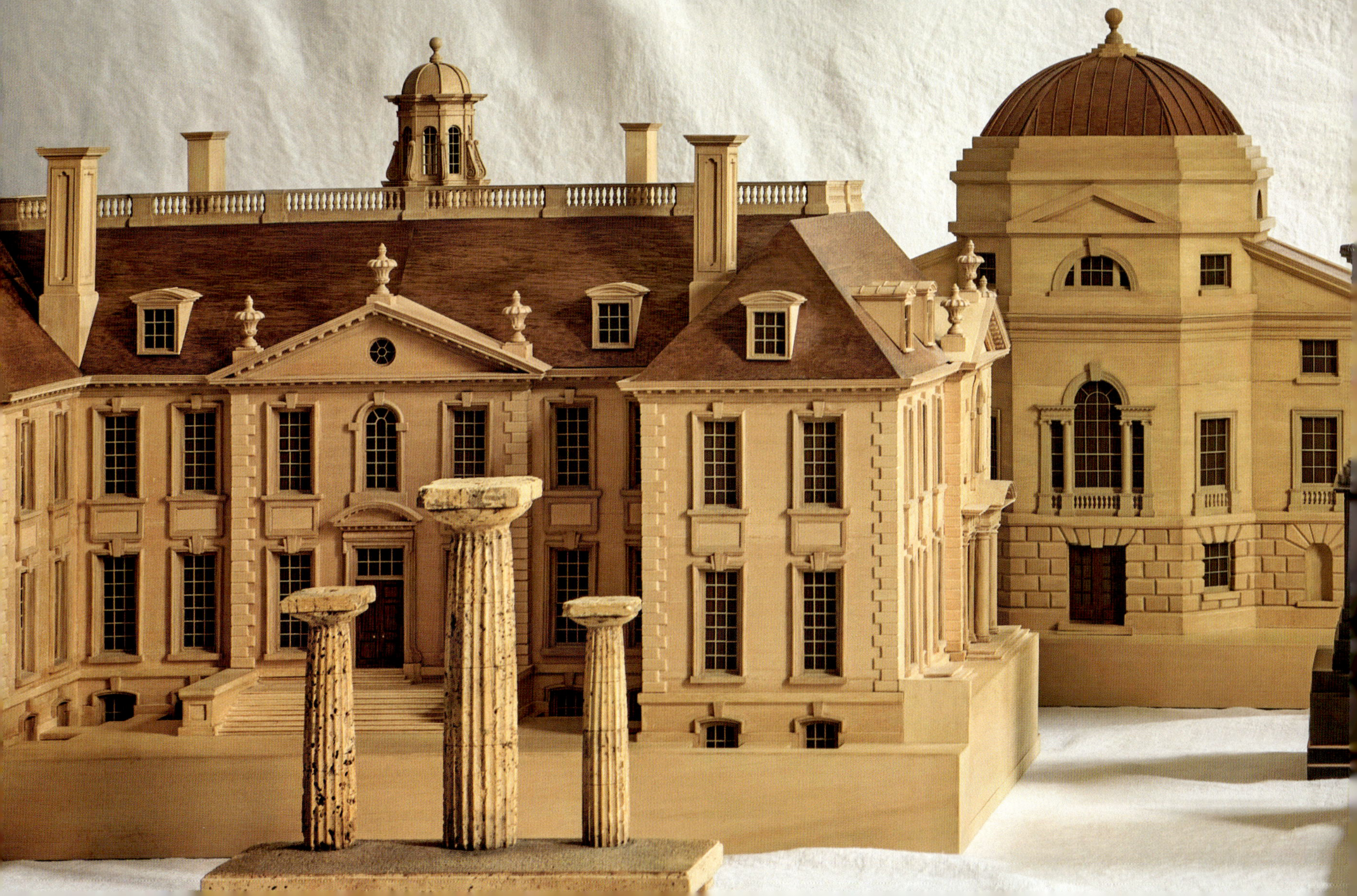

Dieter Cöllen

This book is dedicated to
HIS MAJESTY KING CHARLES III
who has done so much to promote
a humane and beautiful
built and natural
world.

A plaster replica of one of the pair of medals sculpted by Ian Rank-Broadley of His Majesty The King and Her Majesty The Queen, which ornament my building, Royal Pavilion, in Poundbury (see also pages 142–51).

FOREWORD

I first met Ben Pentreath back in 2006 in circumstances which I'll never forget. That year the Moray Estate had invited representatives from the town-planning firm Duany Plater-Zyberk of Miami, including its legendary founder Andrés Duany, to be an integral part of a planning workshop in September where, in a design pressure-cooker environment near Inverness, the DNA of our proposed town of Tornagrain was formulated. Andrés had enlisted Ben, just back from New York and setting up his own practice in London, to join the design team. The ten days of the workshop were an intense yet stimulating and creative time. In the thick of the mayhem was Ben, whose extraordinary talent, creativity and productivity shone out: the faster Andrés tossed design briefs to him, the faster he responded with an endless and beautiful series of townhouses, terraces and cottages. By the last day, a demanding Andrés could think of only one more challenge for Ben: to contrive an entire contiguous high street. In seemingly no time at all, thirty feet of architects tracing paper had been filled with a flawless array of civic buildings, shops and residences. My wife Cathy, myself and the six hundred local people who attended the workshop responded to Ben's work with almost universal enthusiasm; as a result of all this compelling work, the masterplan and design code for Tornagrain were established.

After the workshop we kept in close touch and in due course Ben Pentreath Ltd took on the role of both Tornagrain town planner and architect. Over the years Ben and his team's manifest talents have gained both national and international recognition, and, besides a prominent role in urban developments such as the Duchy of Cornwall's pioneering Poundbury, they are creating some of the twenty-first century's most beautiful houses, both architecturally and decoratively.

This wonderful book gives an insight into Ben's wide breadth of talent, from his ability to visualise and plan an urban environment in three dimensions to his intuitiveness in applying the correct architectural detail. In addition, his masterful juxtaposition of colour, texture and fabric gives even his grandest interiors an intimate sense of harmony and comfort. It is a huge pleasure when Ben, often accompanied by his husband Charlie McCormick, stays with us in Scotland. Besides the serious work of designing a town, there is always plenty of time for fun, laughter and reminiscing over the extraordinary journey we have all been on together.

THE EARL OF MORAY

opposite Knotty-spruce porches on new cottages at Malvina Green, Tornagrain. This high Victorian feature is characteristic of many of the nineteenth-century estate cottages on the Moray Estate, and is part of the local DNA that we have carried forward in the design of the new town.

INTERIORS
THE COLLEGE OF ARMS LONDON

A REFLECTION ON TWO DECADES

It's often easiest to make sense of life by looking in the rear-view mirror. I guess I am now a little beyond halfway through the journey, and it's a nice place to pause for a while and contemplate the scene. If I begin to think about everything that we work on today in our studio, with projects of so many different types and scales in several countries, I can say with certainty that none of it was planned or thought about when I first opened the office twenty years ago. Things have happened incrementally. I had recently returned to London after five blissfully happy years in New York, working for architectural firm Fairfax & Sammons. I had joined the Prince's Foundation for the Built Environment, in a challenging role as an urban and architectural designer, when I received a small repeat fee for some houses that I had designed a year before for a Dorset-based housebuilder. I found myself unexpectedly with enough money in the bank to pay the rent for three months and, without thinking too hard, decided to take the plunge and set up on my own. I took a desk in the corner of a busy architectural studio in Shoreditch and started on a first project: a competition entry for some new houses in Northamptonshire. My client and I were lucky enough to win the competition and I had my first proper job (a good thing, because there really hadn't been a Plan B).

opposite Here I am, standing in our office on Lamb's Conduit Street, a beautiful early eighteenth-century room with wonderful carving on the joinery and a fine plaster ceiling. We uncovered the white marble fireplace under many layers of thick gloss paint. This portrait was taken by my old friend Simon Bevan.

With the benefit of hindsight it is reasonably easy to map out how one project has led to another – very often in a sideways direction – but there was never a grand plan. So much of life is the result of happy accidents: what you might call serendipity. A year after starting, I was asked by my former boss, mentor and still wonderfully close friend, Charles Morris, to help him with the design of a new hotel in the New Forest National Park. That in turn prompted other enquiries. And a year after that I was asked to design significant alterations and extensions to a listed house in the Chiltern Hills, in Oxfordshire, which to this day remains one of my happiest (and largest) projects, and one which was designed to an amazing level of detail and attention because there was a lot of time to work on it.

Slowly, as the office grew, things started to develop in unexpected ways. In 2008, with my great friend Bridie Hall, we opened a little shop in an empty premises around the corner from our office in Bloomsbury. I'd needed some more desks, and this was a means of making extra space. The shop was a 'front' to the office behind. We jokingly used to say that the shop never needed to make any money, and it truthfully was in those days an entirely uncommercial adventure. We never once thought too hard about profit margins or what customers expected, but just maybe because of that, rather than despite it, our little shop quickly flourished and became an unexpected success. After a few months we needed more display space at the back, and the office desks had to squeeze into the back of our main room. I'd like to think that, together, Bridie and I have been charting our course for the last sixteen years in a way that feels different from the normal run-of-the-mill, with a profound set of beliefs (combined with a strong shared sense of humour) that we honed during those early days and have carried forward ever since. We've also lasted a long time, which is no mean feat in the world of London retail.

The shop led to me writing a blog, and the blog to being commissioned to write the first of my books: *English Decoration* (2012), which featured both my own houses and those of many friends. *English Houses* (2016) followed a few years later. By this time, I'd also been lucky enough to take a lease on a beautiful house in West Dorset, which I've lived in for sixteen happy years (the last nine with my wonderful husband Charlie). I'm not quite sure why, but something about this house, and the way I was writing about buildings, chimed with a certain approach to doing them up, and people started asking me to help with interiors as well as architecture, with the furniture and furnishings. This became a whole new route into working on some fabulous buildings – many of them old houses requiring restoration and a new lease of life – and with it has come the discovery of that strange alchemy of ingredients, namely furniture, colours, books and pictures, which creates *atmosphere*, above and beyond the abstract lines of architecture.

All these strands have grown cumulatively. They are the warp and weft of my cloth, and if I tried to remove any one thread, I think the whole piece of fabric would unravel. So, at the end of the first twenty years, the Pentreath Studio is now more than forty people strong, with talented groups of master planners, architects and interior decorators working in three separate but interlinked teams (and a further group of colleagues in the shop and its warehouse). In 2022 the studio became a wholly employee-owned enterprise, and I have been giving a great deal of thought to how it can continue to develop and have a life after me.

In putting together this book of our practice's work, I've felt flashes of anxiety, as you can imagine. I've struggled with the different ways in which to present some of what we are up to: it is hard to categorise an interior designer who is also working for at least a third, if not half, of the time on urban design projects, and vice versa. Just for a start, you can hear my long-suffering editor's question: 'And exactly which shelf of the bookshop should this book sit on?' Even as I write, I'm not *quite* sure of the answer. For me, it is really all about creating environments – be they large or small – in which we can find humanity, beauty, craft, meaning, colour, pattern, comfort, welcome, kindness, authentic detail and a sense of timelessness and history.

I remember so well, when I was probably fifteen years old, picking up that month's copy of the *Architectural Review* in my school's art library. Several pages in, there was an article about a recent building in London by the architect Quinlan Terry, whom I had then never heard of. Almost inevitably, the article was full of derision for what it described as 'pastiche', but for me it was an electric moment to discover that someone was building with stone, mouldings, hipped roofs and sash windows. In the library a few years later I came across the work of Terry's great mentor and master, Raymond Erith, and from there, more books about the continuing tradition of English and American classical design. I realised the things I was interested in were still possible. It's strange to recall that this was a time – in the late 1980s and early '90s – when publications *really* mattered. It was how you found out about things ... in libraries or bookshops (to this day, I cannot walk past a second-hand bookshop without diving in).

When I was sixteen, a careers master at school told me that because I wasn't good at maths or physics, I could never be an architect. I was told to apply to read History at Oxford or Cambridge – well, no interviews ever went worse in my life. I found myself studying Fine Art, and then History of Art, and then History of Architecture, at the University of Edinburgh. I still didn't quite realise that it would be possible for me to make the jump into actual design. I have Charles Morris to thank forever for drawing me down this path.

I say this in closing because perhaps this book is being held, and this page being read, by someone who's not quite sure of themselves, but has an inkling that they'd like to design things or buildings or places. Have faith in your abilities; look, learn, draw and express yourself. Believe, and I am sure it can happen. We are living in unsettled times, when the problems of the world can seem insurmountable, but I am convinced that with the dedication and skill of new generations, life will continue to flourish, and our planet will become better, more resilient, and a more just and beautiful place, if we make it so.

below A design for a new stone temple folly for a site in north Dorset (see also the model on page 4). The building was not constructed.

following pages Our studio in Lamp Office Court, Bloomsbury, London: an early twentieth-century former printing works. When we arrived here it was completely derelict. Now it is filled with creativity, light, life, and plants.

PART ELEVATION of THE ENTRANCE FRONT of FAWLEY HOUSE, OXON

CHAPTER ONE

MY WAY OF THINKING

In thinking about how I work, I'd like to begin with a confession, which is that I often don't like to think too hard at all. This is not to say that at the studio we don't give a huge amount of time, care and attention to the breadth and detail of our work – we do – but more that it is a happy process, with a degree of chance to it, a bit like the best cooking, which is a combination of following good recipes, with a splash of inspiration and sometimes some luck. Those are the dishes we all love to eat and remember.

Revisiting the projects that feature in this book, I've had a chance to think about some of the strands that tie our practice together: a sense of happiness, history, character, place, the whole, colour and imperfection, and an understanding of the different rhythms of time. Clearly, these are eternal themes, which belong to all the best places, buildings and rooms, but it's interesting to reflect on how few architects these days do design with a sense of history, or indeed of place, or of where things are made, and how.

If we consider these ideas in everything we do, we will also end up with buildings and places that have a sense of timelessness, and which are loved. Those buildings, incidentally, without shouting to anyone about how clever they are, quietly become the most sustainable places of all.

Luck comes into the mix, too: the elusive synergy of the right client, planning officer, budget and design ethos – the 'negotiation with life' as I have heard it called. We've been lucky enough to have this more often than not, although in looking at all our office projects, it's hard not to feel a sense of regret for the buildings that haven't happened, as well as joy for those that have. And if this feeling is one that many an architect, decorator or designer who might be reading these pages can share, let's be grateful for the times when things have gone well, and for the people who have made it so.

opposite My pin board in the office. Every time I see an interesting picture on Instagram, I take a screenshot, print it out and pin it up. This is an ever-expanding collage of buildings I love. Next door in our decoration studio is a similar collage for rooms and furniture. I find this process is the best way not only to enjoy the visual stimulation provided by our phones and social media, but also to make the connections between different architectural themes that delight me.

A Sense of Happiness

There is something intuitive about seeking the right approach, but this can be lost by over-thinking. Architecture doesn't need to be torturous, despite the way in which several generations of contemporary architects have been exposed to the anguished training of the post-war architecture schools, often by people who seem to be deeply unhappy (and sometimes rather angry too). The misunderstood hero of Ayn Rand's *The Fountainhead* (1943), the architect as aloof poet or philosopher – these are clothes that don't fit comfortably on me. One of the fortunate things about being a designer who isn't afraid of learning from history – even, frankly, copying from history quite often – is that the whole sum of human creativity becomes a rich well to drink from, a profound and endless pattern book, as opposed to a burden to compete with but never to use. There is lots of laughter in our office every day. It's a happy engagement, this intuitive business of designing good, long-lasting, beautiful places for people to live in. There are arguments from time to time, and sometimes we have to fight for our beliefs and values to be upheld. But even those discussions should be good-natured, because in the end we are all just muddling along trying to do our best.

I love words, but when it comes to design, I am a visual person. On our office wall is a poster quoting Andy Warhol's famous dictum: 'I never read, I just look at pictures'. That is just how I think about buildings, houses and places. They are visual. What do they look like, how do they work? I think this is often a much more important question to ask than 'what do they mean', but so many buildings and cities, and even interiors, have become experiments in meaning rather than in looks, beauty or function.

I am also a person who believes profoundly that the world is a more beautiful and wonderful place *because of* people. It's sometimes easy, faced with the troubles that our planet is assailed by, to forget this. The world is complex, and we have the capacity to bring cruelty, ugliness and disaster wherever we live, but let's not lose track of our immense ability to conserve nature, to protect our natural environment and to create cities, towns, villages, landscapes, houses and rooms: places of the greatest and most incredible long-lasting beauty, and which are truly in a state of equilibrium. We need to have confidence in ourselves as *creators*, a confidence that I find today is ebbing, and which must be retaught and relearnt by new generations, with passion.

opposite Our bothies in Scotland, which you can see more of in the final chapter of this book (pages 340–9). With the buildings' cheery yellow windows and the one's bright red corrugated roof, they are the epitome of architectural happiness for Charlie and me.

A Sense of History

Among her many talents, my mother was a potter. At home in Dorset, I have a beautiful jug that Mum made for me for my twenty-first birthday. It is one of the things I treasure most, with its leaf patterns scrolling around two mysterious birds, their motto tucked in just behind the handle: 'It is the end that crowns us, not the flight'. She worked her whole life totally within the English slipware tradition, that wonderful, robust world of coloured clays and slips, first perfected by Thomas Toft and his contemporaries in the Staffordshire Potteries in the later seventeenth century, and which resonated through the centuries in a living tradition before finding a further revival in the English craft movement of the early twentieth century.

Mum was not well known as a potter. What I love about her pottery is she never once worried about what she was doing, or why. She did what came naturally to her. She did, it is true, make study visits to the Victoria and Albert Museum (V&A), which has remarkable collections of the work of Toft and his family, and by making an appointment in advance you could spend time with these invaluable pieces in the storerooms. She took notes and made drawings of many of those plates, tankards and chargers, but the notes were to do with technique, not design.

She wasn't worried about copying the way something had been done before; she wasn't worried about *not* copying, either. Each time she was asked to make a plate or bowl for someone, she'd sketch out some ideas and think about it, before throwing the pot and then starting the slow, mesmeric task of decorating it with a meticulous pattern that flowed out of her hands as she was working. At the beginning, she never quite knew how she would finish. As a young child, I remember just sitting in her pottery for hours at a time, watching her work. If only architecture could be so effortless! And, I think it should be. At university, in Edinburgh, I was lucky enough to read History of Architecture, where I dipped deep into the rich strains of seventeenth-, eighteenth- and nineteenth-century Scottish classicism, as well as early twentieth-century Vienna and mid-century Los Angeles.

The historian looks at the ancient walls and plans of houses and buildings and tries to determine who they were built by, and for whom, and how; that is all well and good, but for me, I realise now that I was actually on a fantastic mind trip through the past, unencumbered by the baggage that sadly tortured so many of my contemporaries who studied pure architecture, and who were banned by their tutors from making that particular journey. It is easy to value originality, but easier still to overlook the sum of human experience and knowledge. When we are faced with an architectural problem in my office, of any sort – how to detail something, how to resolve a junction between two elements, how to proportion a façade, how big to make a garden square – there is generally nothing that hasn't been beautifully and elegantly solved by an architect or builder in history. You just have to look and learn. In other walks of life, we call that experience. In architecture, we tend to call it pastiche, or cheating.

Call it what you will, I love to draw inspiration from the past, often more directly than you can imagine. Is there anything more wonderful than stepping into the shoes of our ancestors, thinking how they thought, looking at their buildings, learning from them by studying details, and bringing strands of history to life again with authenticity and with a deep sense of historical narrative?

The trick, I find, with history, is to wear its clothes lightly and to celebrate the multifaceted jewels of experience that it has to offer, drawing inspiration where one likes, without becoming suffocated. That is the lesson of my mother's beautiful jug: timeless, crafted, effortless and still, inevitably, unique and of its time.

opposite The slipware jug that my mother made for my twenty-first birthday, one of my most treasured possessions.

PENTREATH·1992·

PRAISE
LORD.

A Sense of Character

There are lots of architects and decorators we can think of who have a distinctive 'look'. You can identify their projects a mile off, whether a building or a room. There is nothing wrong with this at all. In fact, I often look at the work of many of my friends with a sense of awe at the coherent way in which they build the narrative of their designs.

But, at the end of the day, it is not how I like to work. For one site, we might be working in an austere Palladian language, and elsewhere in a happy and overblown Victorian guise. We could be designing rooms with modern furniture and a contemporary sensibility, gentle and restrained, for one client, while for another we could be plunging headlong into colour and pattern. For me, each building, house, room and person has its own character, and my job is to try and tease this out and to celebrate it. I want everything we do to sing with the unique personality of the place.

I sometimes explain to new clients how important they are in the process of creating this story. The house that you see on pages 194–205 – at Chettle, in Dorset – was one of the happiest projects of my career, for one of the loveliest clients you could ever hope to work with. We were in synergy every step of the way, from the choices of colours, patterns and wallpapers to the placement of things; of where to go for it, and where to hold back. And Tom and Rosamond have subsequently become kind and generous friends.

But the story of my work at Chettle had begun earlier. When the house was first sold, it was bought by an equally lovely couple, but very much younger, who were thrilled with and daunted by their new home. They knew that I knew the house and called on me to come and help, which I was excited to do. We started by developing ideas and beginning to orchestrate the approach to Historic England and planning officers. We also – as always – discussed costs. It became clear that the budget was going to need to be very significant, more than my clients had imagined. I will never forget the thoughtful call I received saying that they were worried they had made a mistake. It would be a good thing in life if more people had that reflective ability to know when they were getting out of their comfortable depth. We all agreed that the best way to proceed was to see if they could sell the house on, quietly and quickly, before the situation became really serious and stressful, which, with consummate ease, they did: Tom and Rosamond gratefully picked up the baton, and I was so incredibly happy, a few months later, to be asked back (that really was a twist of fate).

My first clients had completely contrasting ideas from Tom and Rosamond: excellent ideas, but in no way similar. The house would look vastly different now if this story had proceeded in another direction. Yet, it would have been the same house, with the same interior decorator, but nothing would have been the same. The only change in the ingredients was our client. That's the magical thing about a person's character: each one is unique. And it's the most important card in the pack for me.

opposite At our flat in London, a bucket of riotous dahlias explodes with colour. Some favourite mugs are on the table. There is an eclectic mix here that speaks of my own taste, but especially of Charlie's. However, you could imagine decorating this room in a completely different way for a different person, and that wouldn't be wrong. Each room must respect the building, but more importantly those who are going to live in it.

A Sense of Place

When I am working on any project, of any scale, there is the crucial instant when you are first visiting the site and you sense that spark of what might happen here. Sometimes, you might be standing in an empty room of an unloved country house; sometimes, in a small city flat; or in a wide-open field that one day will become the site of a new town; or the valley that will be the setting of someone's new house and its surrounding landscape.

In each case, one's mind immediately starts whirring with the possibilities. Quite often these days, first site visits seem to be crowded with people from many disciplines – it is one of the rules of modern life. But you'll often find me standing a bit away from everyone else. This is not because I'm being unfriendly or rude. No. I'm trying to listen to the *soul* of that building, or of that piece of land, perhaps bouncing around ideas with the landscape architect. Today, there are so many distractions for us all, compounded by a world in which visual imagery bombards our eyes constantly, that I wonder, one day, if the clamour will be so great that you'll have to get right down on your hands and knees, and press your ear to the ground to hear the heartbeat, the whisper, of what it is we should be thinking about?

Once you've caught that whisper, I find the rest falls into place. Here are the questions I think about: what is going to feel most inevitable here; what is going to have the greatest sense of permanence, of repose, of being most settled within its landscape? What building is going to belong best upon this site; what materials, what forms, what mass, what scale, what idea and sense of narrative are we wishing to convey? In a house: what decoration is going to feel most comfortable, what will chime most beautifully with the architecture, and resonate with the lives of those who will dwell here? These questions are not asked individually, but simultaneously reverberate around my mind.

Like catching the scent of a flower on a breeze, the germ of the idea might be transitory: miss it, and it can disappear forever. That is why one needs to concentrate so hard to catch it. But it's like finding a little seed, and then watering it, protecting it and nourishing it – giving it structure and support, and letting it grow into a life entirely of its own, which will hopefully last long after we have all gone.

In 1993 Angela King and Sue Clifford (founders of the charity Common Ground, which campaigns for 'Local Distinctiveness') wrote a thought-provoking essay called 'Losing Your Place', which examines some of these themes:

> *The main players fall silent, the filming is over, the recording is finished, but the sound technician has hushed everyone to get some 'atmos'. Coughs, car noise echoing off the warehouses, birdsong, boards creaking, trees breathing in the wind, these are the sounds of the everyday, so particular to this place, that to cut the film and add studio voiceovers needs an underlay of this local atmosphere in order to ensure continuity and authenticity.*
>
> *That elusive particularity, so often undervalued as 'background noise', is as important as the stars. It is the richness we take for granted. How do we know where we are in time and space? How do we understand ourselves in the world?*

I've never forgotten the moment, as a student at Edinburgh University, sitting in the kitchen of our lofty flat in the New Town, when I first read the Common Ground 'Manifesto in Praise of Local Distinctiveness'. It was May Day 1991, and the charity had taken an eye-catching full-page advertisement in *The Independent* newspaper. From there I read all their work and writing, and it taught me the beginnings of a philosophy that I have endeavoured to live by ever since.

opposite An autumnal morning on one of our walks at home in Littlebredy, Dorset. Charlie and I must have walked this hill thousands of times now, and every day it feels different.

A Sense of the Whole

There was a moment when the entire sum of architectural knowledge could be contained in maybe ten books. A prominent architect of the late seventeenth century might have had a few sparse volumes on his shelves; he learnt in a manner that is unfamiliar to us today, part of a living tradition of apprenticeship, studying geometry, nature, astronomy and the classical orders in the most practical way. The word *architect* meant something completely different then, compared with today's meaning in the professionalised, specialised world in which we live.

I am always struck by the fact that so many of the buildings that we cherish most were built by people whom today we might call uneducated: people who couldn't read, or write, or spell, save perhaps to mark their name. But they belonged to that living, breathing tradition of building, of stone carving, bricklaying, joinery, glazing, lead plumbing or plastering, that had no need of words and schedules, and they innately understood how to proportion, how to detail and how to build. These craftspeople managed, without the aid of fossil fuel or technology, to create some of the most transcendently beautiful examples of architecture ever made.

The first true classical architect in England, Inigo Jones, belonged to a tradition that saw him equally at home designing stage scenery and costumes, ephemeral festivities for masques, and those early essays in pure Palladian classicism that must have looked so alien to English eyes. A century later, William Kent was as much artist and furniture designer as he was architect. Robert Adam and his brothers designed anything: urban squares, developments, sensational façades and plans, ceilings, sofas, upholstery, door escutcheons. Nothing was too large or too small for their attention. Every element of the city, of the picturesque landscape, of the house and its furnishings was there to be designed and considered, in a rich, non-prescriptive way. Looking at the original Adam drawings in the archive of the Sir John Soane's Museum in London, each sheet fizzes with the excitement of design and colour, of light and shade and composition that swept across all scales of their creativity.

opposite A plaster ceiling at a house in Oxfordshire (you can see the stair hall on page 163). Made by the superbly skilled hand of Geoffrey Preston, the plasterwork was inspired by Preston's and my collaborative research, with references (among others) to beautiful Mompesson House, Salisbury.

We live in a world of ever-increasing specialisation and expertise. No one suffers this more than architects, but we have created this rod for our own backs. We become experts in specific fields. Our minds become filled with technical solutions and building regulations; our urban developments are defined by turning radiI and bin lorry routes and local authority highways 'adoptable standards'. And we all go along with it.

I draw huge inspiration from William Chambers, Kent and Adam, those pre-nineteenth-century, pre-specialist architects whose vivid imaginations sprawled uncontrollably across so many spheres. They focused on what mattered: the eternal, transcendent qualities that make life worth living. In a world where large firms now exist purely to design a client's audio-visual system, or to meet obligations under health and safety legislation, or that specialise in the care-home sector (nearly always creating buildings that would suck all joy out of me if I had to live in them), it's all the more vital to keep searching for that spark of what our task is all about: designing things of all scales. Our eye jumps from a full-size panel detail to plasterwork, from furnishings and fabrics to buildings; from streets and squares to the structure of a whole town, and back again, in a heartbeat.

This sense of the whole is something that architecture needs to recapture – a whole that, incidentally, is always greater than the sum of the parts, and where *beauty*, *wit*, *intrigue* and *proportion* are our watchwords, as we try to create an enduring frame for this messy thing called life.

A Sense of Colour

There is no right or wrong about colour, which is one of the wonderful things about life. Honestly, whatever anyone tells you – there are no rules regarding colour! Imagine that. The world of classical and traditional architecture that I inhabit is, by contrast, very rules-based: there really are right and wrong ways of doing things, whether it be the placement of a moulding, the detailing of elements or the handling of materials. Understand the rules, and a lot falls into place. Edwin Lutyens, that inspirational genius, talked brilliantly about playing 'the great game', but even games need parameters. Even those who break the rules of architecture (and he most certainly was one of them) need to know what they are and how to break them. So maybe this is why I'm so experimental with colour.

While there are great traditions we can work within, these are sometimes misunderstood. There is a general sense that the early Georgians lived with earthy, muted tones, whereas we know that nothing quickened their hearts more than an electric blue or an emerald green; the Regency eye loved bright saturation and the Victorians went mad for new colours (never more so than for mauve, invented as a chemical dye in 1859). Even international modernism, which was transmitted to the world through black-and-white photographs, is easily thought to be without colour, whereas the historian of the twentieth century knows that it was a veritable riot of pink, yellow, blue, red and green.

How do I think about colour? An awful lot comes down to intuition and feeling. Yes, I will draw inspiration from my historical experience, but did David Hicks, one of the greatest colourists of the twentieth century, or Billy Baldwin or Josef Frank worry about that? There are certain colours I return to time and again, as the sharp-eyed will note in this book: I love sludgy olive greens, burnt orange, turquoise blue, egg-yolk yellow. At home, in Dorset, I'd started life with a pale grey wall in my sitting room that after the second winter definitely needed warming up. I decided on pink but couldn't find the perfect tone. After some disastrous home experiments, I called in Patrick Baty, who remains one of my absolute go-to colourists in all of our projects. Together, Patrick and I concocted just the right pink. My sitting room was photographed, and he began to be asked to make it more widely. It narrowly avoided being called Pentreath Pink, and we settled on the term Parsonage Pink, which sits very nicely in Patrick's 'Odd Useful Colours' range.

A lot is down to personal sensibility. We all react to colour in our own way. I remember meeting a client with a beautiful old house in Norfolk with a long, low-ceilinged, north-facing entrance hall running the entire length of the building. I felt it would benefit from a rich colour and suggested what was my immediate, intuitive hunch: would a warm, strong blue be a good antidote to the cold Norfolk light – a fine colour for an excellent collection of mahogany furniture and paintings to hang against? 'But I really don't like blue', she replied – and you can't argue with that! So, we settled on a different palette entirely, which worked just as well. There's no right or wrong.

Then there's the effect of colours in combination: astonishing Augustus Pugin block prints from Watts & Co. or eighteenth-century patterns by Adelphi Paper Hangings, or, at the other end of the scale, the magical (and free) ingredient of colour in our housing development projects, such as a terrace of black-and-white houses in Scotland enlivened by a palette of brightly coloured front doors.

Over many years now, I've been known for my embrace of bright colour, a quality in my life only enhanced by my marriage to Charlie, who is the true instigator of our yellow gloss paint in the kitchen in Dorset, or the brilliant lime green of the flower room in London. I am, however, just as happy working with the quietest palette imaginable, pure white, or with sugar tones. Wouldn't the world be joyless without colour?

opposite Sugary tones for a fine Regency house in the south of England – an interior defined by a powerful yet balanced sense of colour: not quite historical, not quite modern.

CHAPTER TWO

IN THE CITY

CHAPTER TWO

IN THE CITY

Why do I love cities so much? I suppose it started with the moment that I overcame the fears of childhood and became my own, independent person, moving to university in the thrilling, austere city of Edinburgh, sharply lit by clear northern light; followed by months travelling in Athens, Istanbul, Aleppo, Damascus and then down to Delhi and India; and visiting the great European cities of Rome, Florence, Venice, Berlin and Seville. Or was it the times after university, when I left my little village in Norfolk and went down to London for weekends with friends and had fun and got into trouble?

previous pages A drawing of our Royal Crescent of new houses in Truro, Cornwall, designed in 2009. You can see photographs of the completed project on pages 60–5.

Yes, of course, all of this, but I think my love affair with the idea of the city *really* began twenty-five years ago, when I moved to New York. I lived for eighteen months in the tiniest two-room apartment in Greenwich Village, on Bank Street, on the top floor of a nineteenth-century brownstone. The building was crumbling and was filled with tenants, in rent-controlled units, who the new owner was desperately (and rather unsuccessfully) trying to evict. It was the last year of the last century and I found myself in delirious New York at a moment when America was seemingly boundless in its confidence and self-belief, untroubled still by problems that only the foresighted could have glimpsed on the horizon.

I loved discovering the layers, the palimpsest, of beautiful old New York City, which was simultaneously so modern and energetic, and yet I found the feeling of history here far closer to the surface than in sprawling London, forever redeveloping itself in unnecessary ways. I lived and loved and stayed up all night, and wandered into the office after very little sleep and somehow managed to work the long hours that were needed. On coming home from a late night out with friends, six weeks after my arrival, I was pistol-whipped at my doorstep. I survived the experience, maybe with a heightened sense of caution. I spent the summer on Long Island and in Coney Island, and briefly for a glorious week on Mount Desert Island, Maine. Back in the city, I sweltered in the heat and humidity that was hitherto unimaginable. I adored New York. That first autumn, Mum and Dad came to stay, and found a son transformed. Perhaps that is why we love cities so much: in their very anonymity, their hugeness, they have the power to transform and rewrite the page that was drafted in the town or village in which so many of us started life.

Two years later I had moved to west SoHo, to another tiny apartment, which was six-feet wide at its narrowest point. I adored living there. From my bed, I had a wonderful distant view to the Empire State Building, seeming to float above the rest of New York. I will never forget that crisp September morning when, from the clear autumnal blue sky, the horror of the 9/11 terror attacks emerged. That night, the city dense with smoke and sorrow and the smell of burning, and the air filled with sirens wailing, I lay in bed, awake with fear, and it felt as if the city – the very idea of the city – would never recover; a feeling that repeated itself in a different frame twenty years later as cities around the globe found themselves silent, empty, full of the fear of the Covid pandemic. But they rebound. We are social animals. We know that we are better together. And cities will be with us, sprawling, messy, uncontrollable, ugly, beautiful, for as long as there are people on earth. I love cities: their endless sense of possibility, of change, of history, of danger and of vision.

Our studio belongs in the heart of the city, and like so much of London, we're just the tiniest fragment of a huge and ever-changing place, but here too is a palimpsest. We work on Lamb's Conduit Street, in the heart of Bloomsbury, a street that has evolved yet retains a powerful connection to its early eighteenth-century origins, when farmland and market gardens subsumed to development as London underwent its first massive expansion. Mr Lamb's conduit brought in fresh drinking water to the city, and that's how the street got its name. At the northern end is the site of the remarkable Foundling Hospital, one of the great charitable institutions of early Georgian London; its railings and entrance gates remain, although the hospital is long gone.

My first office was in a handsome 1720s drawing room on the first floor of a townhouse looking over Lamb's Conduit Street, with an extraordinary plaster ceiling and a fine marble chimney-piece that we uncovered from under layers of thick paint (see page 10). We still keep that room for meetings and lectures. Our main studio today is next door, housed in a rabbit warren of spaces that were constructed in the early twentieth century over the garden yard of another early eighteenth-century townhouse. Originally a printing works (effectively a large, top-lit industrial shed), the building has undergone numerous uses in the last sixty years; we are merely the latest inhabitants. We've done our best to insulate, but the structure is old and leaky and rather eccentric. It is, however, a wonderful, living, breathing example of adaptable reuse that I believe is at the heart of the most sustainable way that architecture can work (see pages 14–15). It is a microcosm of how cities will survive and flourish in the future. When I see images in the architectural press of huge, shiny, energy-efficient office towers, I think of our 1720s townhouse room, infinitely versatile, and how it's already three hundred years old. I wonder which building will still be here in another three hundred years. We all intuitively know the answer.

In the Spirit of Bloomsbury

BLOOMSBURY, LONDON, 2012–

This is where Charlie and I live, on the upper floors of an old Georgian townhouse, with our windows above the trees, overlooking the green and leafy Queen Square. It is a fascinating place to live, home to us for the last decade, and to the Art Workers' Guild since 1913.

The Guild is a club for artists, architects, artisans and sculptors; it was established in 1884 by young followers of William Morris. By the turn of the century the Guild had become the most powerful voice in the burgeoning Arts and Crafts Movement of Edwardian England, and in 1913 the members grouped together to buy a permanent home for the club, in a handsome 1720s townhouse on Queen Square in Bloomsbury. The Guild offices were on the ground and first floors, and the upper levels were converted into apartments.

I was lucky enough to move into the top-floor flat in 2012, and a few years later, Charlie and I were able to take over the floor below when our downstairs neighbour moved to Paris. We have kept our living room and kitchen upstairs, as they were. Down below we have our new bedroom, in a low-ceilinged, bolection-panelled room that is the most comfortable place in which I've ever slept. There's another panelled bedroom and – greatest of luxuries in London – Charlie's flower room, painted in an electric shade of lime green, which doubles up as a bar. Often, he will drive up from Dorset with buckets of flowers from the garden, which then spill out of the old Belfast sink we installed.

The end wall of our living room is covered by a map of London, the so-called Rocque Plan, which was published in 1746 by the cartographer John Rocque. It is a wonderful thing. I'd owned this copy, printed in the 1970s, for some time, and there was a moment when I suddenly realised it would fit perfectly here (and I mean *perfectly*, to the nearest inch, height and width).

On the map, on what was then the northern edge of London, you will find Queen Square, completed on three sides, open to the north. Like its neighbours, the grand villas and townhouses of Great Ormond Street, with their long pleasure gardens stretching north, the square overlooked open countryside: Rocque's map illustrates in great detail a patchwork of market gardens and small farms. And thus London stayed for about a hundred years, as new development went west. It was not until the turn of the nineteenth century that new streets were built to the north. Fifty years later, William Morris was living on Great Ormond Street; his studio, for several decades in the mid-nineteenth century, was almost next door, at No. 26 Queen Square. I find it magical to imagine Morris and his family walking past our building each morning and evening: inspiration in the very pavements beneath our feet and the heartbeat of history every day.

opposite A view from our bedroom to the dressing room beyond. The bedroom is painted in Papers and Paints 'Cambridge Blue', which contrasts beautifully with the orange 'Vase' wallpaper designed by David Hicks. The ikat lampshade was made by Melina Blaxland-Horne.

following pages Our sitting room on the upper floor of the flat. At one end of the room is a map wall with John Rocque's famous 'Plan of London' perfectly filling the space. At the other end is a fine Edwardian fireplace with heavily figured marble and a wonderful lacquer surround. Tabletop clutter includes a ceramic banana – given to us by Bridie Hall – which looks like it's on the brink of going off.

(1)
(2)
(3)
(4)
(5)
(6)

cahiers d'art
AMY MERRICK
tom bianchi

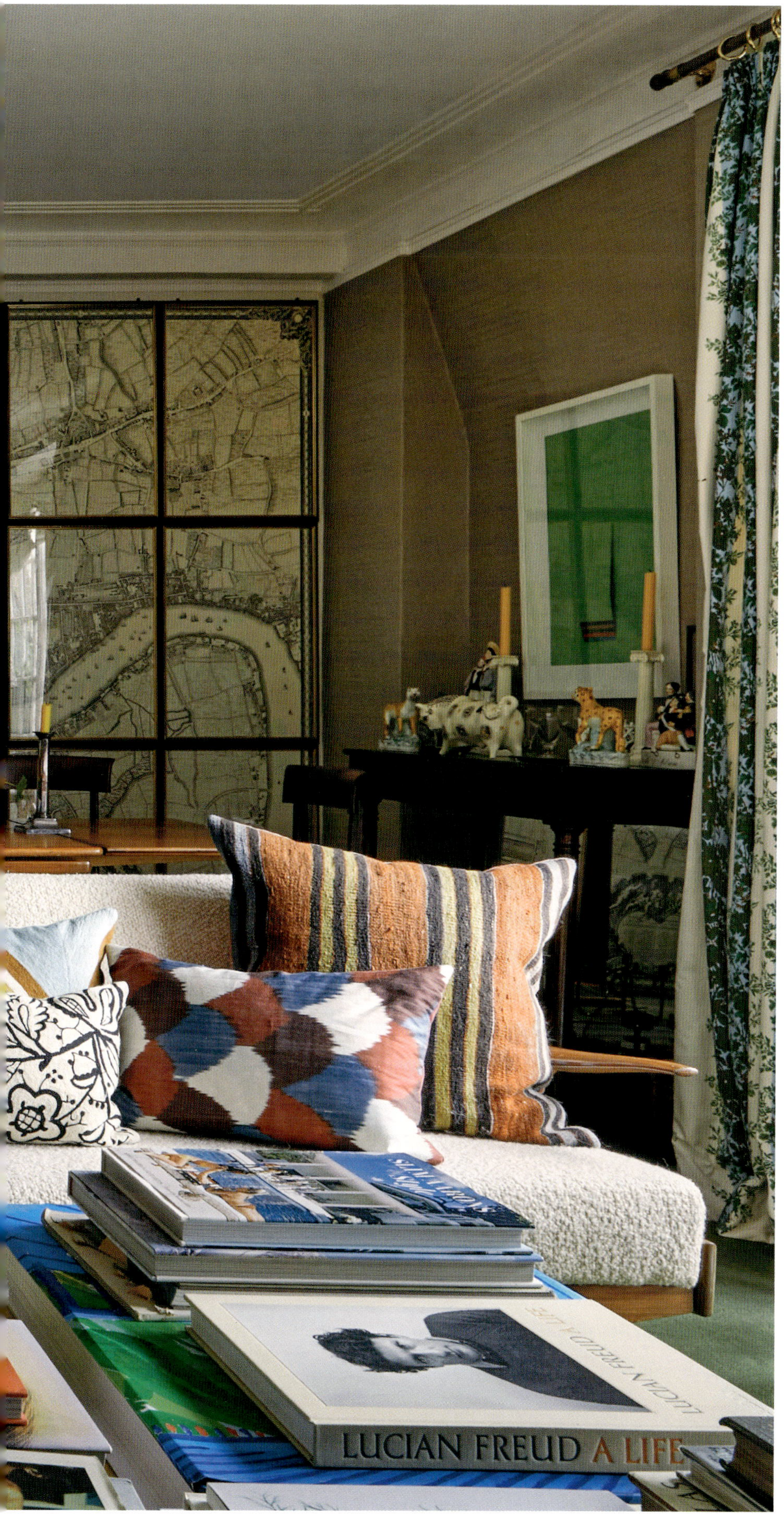
LUCIAN FREUD A LIFE

JOHN DERIAN

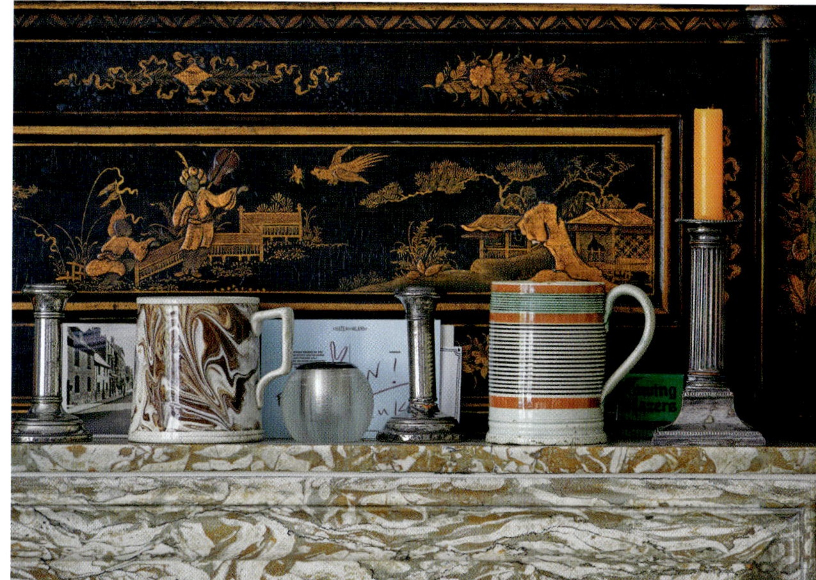

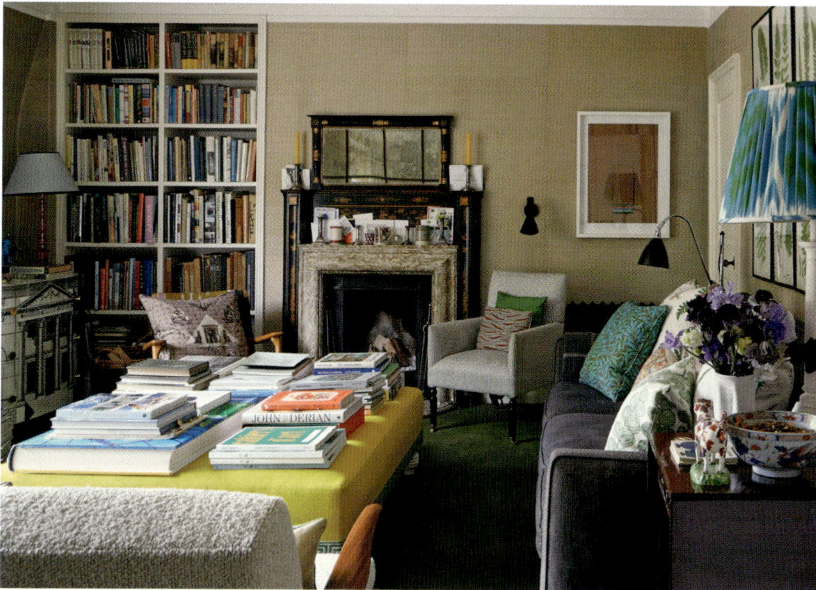

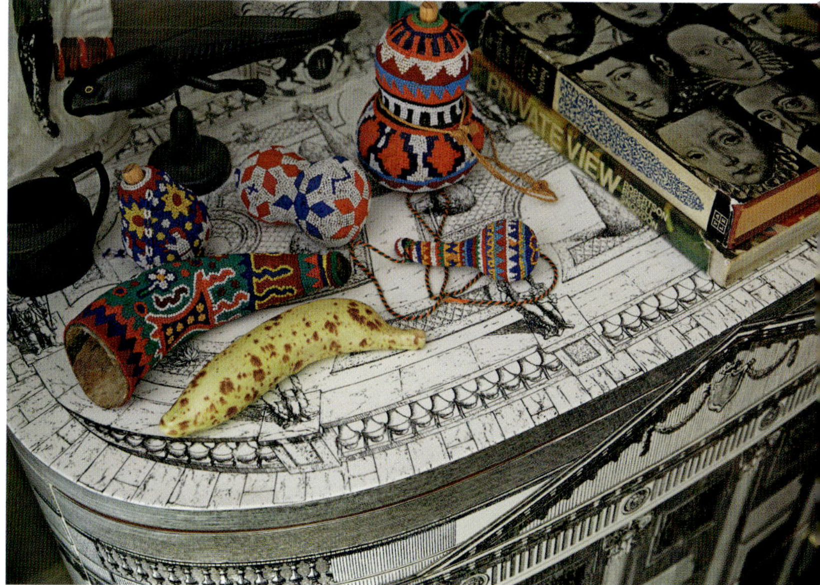

PRIVATE VIEW

MONS
ARTHINGS
PAY ME?
Bailey
W RICH
HAT BE?
NOW
ANDLE
UR HEAD
p chop
S DEAD
HARE &
BURKE

opposite Top left: a view into our kitchen, with bright orange 'Mikado' walls from Papers and Paints, and a resin lamp and yellow lampshade from Marianna Kennedy in the foreground. Top right and bottom left: our bedroom – I bought the extensive collection of Penguin paperbacks from Joe Pearson of Design For Today. Bottom right: our guest bathroom in Zoffany's 'Richmond Park' wallpaper designed by Peter Gomez.

right This guest bedroom is in Soane Britain's 'Seaweed Lace' wallpaper. Lulu Lytle, who owns Soane, introduced Charlie and me. Reflected in the mirror is a drawing of tulips by Oisin Byrne. The jug is newly made by Sussex Lustreware.

above This corridor leading to a guest bedroom is painted in 'HC-70' from Papers and Paints. We bought the pictures in a junk shop. I've owned the old mahogany chair since I was at Edinburgh University, purchased from James Scott Antiques on Dundas Street.

above This guest room has the four-poster bed made by my grandparents, with specially coloured toile curtains by Christopher Moore and a vivid turquoise-blue lining. The bedspread is 'Mortefontaine' by Pierre Frey. The framed botanical prints are from Pentreath & Hall.

following pages Our flower room is painted in a vivid lime green from Dulux. We installed the old Belfast sink, and Charlie found the yellow-and-white fabric in a junk shop. Most weeks in the summer Charlie will drive up from Dorset with buckets of flowers both for the flat and to give to friends.

with Dave Gelly
Old Tennis Shoes

A House on the Park

REGENT'S PARK, LONDON, 2020–2023

Chester Terrace has perhaps the most beautiful of all the crisp stucco façades that surround Regent's Park, the wonderful green expanse laid out by John Nash and the Prince Regent as the centrepiece of their 'Metropolitan Improvements' in early nineteenth-century London.

Nash was the most renowned of the Regency architects. I admire his work so much, for its *joie de vivre*, confidence and sheer exuberance. I sense that, unlike the bookish John Soane, here was a man who just loved life. In the park, Nash's greatest composition of all, he dashed off remarkable schemes for huge palace-fronted terraces, set against a frame of verdant nature. It was a vision of fluidity and complexity, unmatched elsewhere in London (or, for that matter, in any European city that I know). Chester Terrace, announced by two Corinthian triumphal arches at either end, has always struck me as the finest of these palace fronts. How thrilling it was, then, when Rupert Cunningham, the studio's senior design director, was asked by friends to help with the restoration of one of the townhouses, recently inherited from a revered grandmother.

The house, last renovated sixty years ago, had considerable style – the sort of place that in one sense you could happily just move into. But as is so often the case, the wiring and plumbing were in disarray, and some terrible things had happened here since the building was bombed and largely gutted during the Blitz. Rupert's friends, with their very young family, wanted to live in a way that was slightly different from granny's, bringing the kitchen out of the gloom, creating new bathrooms and children's bedrooms, and most excitingly of all, making a new roof garden with astonishing views above the treetops. It was the sort of invigorating restoration that we love to carry out, Rupert working also with our decoration studio to provide help with colours and furnishings.

Old pictures and furniture have found new places; the architecture is completely revived. New cornices and joinery have been detailed with the fine, restrained, early nineteenth-century quality that is perhaps the hallmark of Rupert's aesthetic; modern services and plumbing introduced in a completely seamless and delicate way; and the whole house redecorated in glowing, jewel-like tones of sapphire, azure and warm saffron yellow.

Today, this is the happiest home you can imagine, filled with the sounds of young feet tearing up and down the slender neoclassical staircase from basement to attic bedrooms. It is a magical place in which to grow up, with the dreamlike park and the zoo on the doorstep: a townhouse from a storybook, filled with adventures yet to be written. The frame has just been set. That's our job. Now the real fun begins.

opposite A detail of the dining room with the ethereal mural painted by Alasdair Peebles and a 'Pelham' fireplace from Jamb. The mirror, designed with a shell keystone, is from Jeremy Rothman.

opposite Nash's rich façade of Chester Terrace, with punchy Corinthian columns and a triumphal arch at each end.

right The entrance hall and stairs are painted in 'Berrington Blue', an archive colour from Farrow & Ball. The Gothick cornice is original. We installed a new Portland stone floor with black slate cabochons.

following pages The dining room, with Peebles's classical mural contrasting beautifully with the marble-topped Saarinen table and 1960s Danish dining chairs. Simple linen blinds filter the light.

opposite A view into the new kitchen that we designed, with cabinets painted in 'Minster Green' by Farrow & Ball, and a strong Arabescato marble backsplash. The range hood is in aged zinc. We painted the hallway doors in a delicate Wedgwood blue with the carved ovolo mouldings picked out in crisp white, in homage to the entrance hall at Kenwood House.

right A view from the upper floor looking down to the first-floor drawing room. The stair carpet, from the 'Westbourne' range by Peter Page, is in a bespoke dyed golden colour.

above The drawing room has an ebonised games table and chairs, as well as a gallery hang of inherited and bought pictures on the south wall. The George Sherlock sofa, in the foreground, is upholstered in 'Wheat Flower' by Bennison.

opposite The tall-ceilinged drawing room, looking towards the fireplace. Nash's huge floor-to-ceiling windows overlook Regent's Park. The sofa is upholstered in a yellow linen by Prelle, and the curtains are in 'Red Oak Stripe' by Michael S. Smith. The abstract painting over the fireplace is by Albert Irvin. The Georgian mantelpiece was installed in the 1960s.

above The new roof garden that we created, with a glazed box that slides back above the staircase. Stripy deckchairs make this a happy place to spend the day and evening. The planting is by Caroline Comber.

opposite The guest bedroom walls are lined in a brown-hessian wallpaper, and the simple cotton ticking curtains are from Ian Mankin. A woven-jute floor is by Alternative Flooring. These materials are made special by our clients' 1960s 'Napoleon' painting by Spanish artist Eduardo Arroyo, neoclassical chest of drawers, campaign chair and Egyptian bust: an eclectic mix of things that brings a vibrant personality to this corner of the house.

A New Crescent for a Small City

TRURO, CORNWALL, 2009

Truro, in the far west of England, is not quite the smallest of Britain's cities, but it has a discernible feeling of being pocket-scaled, nestling in the bowl of hills all around, with the late Victorian cathedral towering over streets of classical houses.

We were given a commission to design a new development for the Duchy of Cornwall, the ancient estate of the Prince of Wales. The site was identified as part of a larger project, by Cornwall Council, to build the eastern section of the city's Park & Ride system, a measure to reduce traffic. Decades of sprawling house-building to the west of Truro have created something of a dystopian problem for the city, swamped as it is by cars in the rush hours at the start and end of the day. A public transport scheme was installed to the west, but in order to reach capacity, a site on the east needed to be established.

The Duchy owned an important, narrow triangle of agricultural land that was proven, by sophisticated traffic modelling, to be the best potential location. Discussions inched forward. So often the ingredients of these city transport schemes create places that feel austere and bleak. With its comprehensive understanding of traditional placemaking, the Duchy was determined to consider a different approach. Where everything is disaggregated and poorly thought through, there's no doubt that it could feel like 'anywhere'. Working closely with my friend Ben Bolgar of the Prince's Foundation, I was determined to make it a 'somewhere': to give this part of the city a meaningful sense of place.

The development faces east over open countryside at the head of a tight wooded valley. I will never forget my first visit. It felt to me that the site demanded something simple, powerful, that would provide an 'edge' between the city and the countryside beyond: a building with a single, uncomplicated roof profile, which would embrace the astonishing distant views to the east. The idea of a crescent was born out of the land. Behind was a small garden square of terraced and detached houses.

As is so often the way, the scheme was controversial and there was much local interest. Planning was finally granted and another few years passed before construction started. Now, as the sun rises on another clear day, one is tempted to ask, 'what was all the fuss about', because this is a place that feels as if it will be here, a part of this wonderful ancient city and landscape, for hundreds of years to come.

opposite Looking east as the sun rises, a view of the new iron lantern brackets that we designed and had made, closely inspired by those on Great Pulteney Street, Bath. Rob Illingworth, the studio's master-planning director, and I measured those fixtures in the pouring rain one afternoon in Bath. We tend to find that measuring historical examples carefully is the best way to get new details right. Not every detail is perfect, but it has the right scale and flavour.

following pages The new Royal Crescent, as the sun rises on a summer morning. There is something so simple and compelling about the crescent form, and it was a wonderful commission to create this new edge to the city, with its distant views to the countryside beyond.

WK69 GJU

opposite and right Behind the crescent are a number of two-storey properties laid out around a square that will soon house a market garden, playground and park. The rendered houses are based carefully on examples in Lemon Street, Truro, with their parapet walls stepping up the hill. A parking mews sits behind the crescent, with two-storey garages with flats above. The materials palette is kept intentionally simple, relying on colour and local stone.

A House of Collections

BLOOMSBURY, LONDON, 2010–

In all of late Georgian Bloomsbury, nowhere is more synonymous with the Bloomsbury Group than Gordon Square, where we find such a contrast between Thomas Cubitt's austerely heavy Greek revival façades of the 1820s and the fertile ideas that bounced around these walls a century later.

Here we are in Gordon Square, a few houses down from the former home of sisters Virginia and Vanessa Stephen (later Virginia Woolf and Vanessa Bell) and the setting for the famous Bloomsbury gatherings held on the first Thursday of the month, frequented by Leonard Woolf, Lytton Strachey, Duncan Grant, John Maynard Keynes, Roger Fry and the rest.

Just along the tree-shaded pavement is this handsome building, which the University of London was selling on: well looked after, but tired, and with much loss of original features. My clients were among some of our very first when I opened the decoration studio. Americans, but with a profound sense of Englishness, and with a relationship to the unique qualities of this crucible of modern ideas and taste, they approached me with a simple proposition: they wanted to restore their house slowly, over a number of years, a room at a time, with no sense of hurry but with a great sense of richness and drama.

As we got to know one another, I realised that they have a special sort of kindness and generosity, to each other, to their circle of friends and to this house, which they love so much. We have restored every inch of the building: stripping plaster ceilings over-painted by the heavy institutional paintbrush over the decades; clearing layers of gloss paint to reveal the original stone staircase; and removing carpet tiles and lino to expose tightly butt-jointed stone-flagged floors. We have reintroduced Greek revival fireplaces, where the originals had been lost, and cleaned centuries of soot off the white marble chimneypieces that were extant. We've replaced horrible modern floors and terrible contemporary windows. We've rewired and replumbed and breathed new life into these old bones.

The process of creating a house together over the last decade was not for the faint-hearted. From the moment I stepped into the monotonous unrestored interiors, with their whiff of decades of university bleach-cleaning in the air, my collaborators were enthused with the idea of establishing a richly hued world that would provide a backdrop to their fine collection of early photographs, impressive library of books and sculpture, much of it with a subversive gay spirit, and which would evoke an atmosphere of many eras. The idea of Bloomsbury was alive again, but infused now with a more mystical spirit, of the late nineteenth century, of Oscar Wilde and Aubrey Beardsley, and the aesthetic movement. It's a house designed to look best of all by candlelight, at a boisterous dinner party surrounded by the sparkling glazed walls of the dining room, or within the rich terracotta of the huge first-floor drawing room, filled anew with conversation, laughter and ideas.

opposite We found this nineteenth-century glazed-oak bookcase, now filled with volumes. The studio commissioned David Coryndon to create an additional perfectly matching pair of bookcases (see pages 70–1). In the foreground is an ottoman covered in Morris & Co.'s 'Vine', from the Queen Square collection that I designed for Sanderson. The atmosphere of this room is intended to evoke the heady mood of a Victorian collector's library.

following pages In the ground-floor dining room we glazed the walls in an intense, ink-blue colour, which sparkles at night when lit by candlelight. We used our clients' existing dining table and covered the chairs in a turquoise horsehair. The curtains are in an Egyptian revival toile by Pierre Frey. The mirror, one of a pair, and the 'Onslow' fireplace surround, with its heavy Greek revival proportions, are all from Jamb. The photographs are by Robert Mapplethorpe and Lisette Model.

MOORE
SCULPTURE TODAY
DAVID HICKS
GILBERT & GEORGE
Millais
TURKS
ARMENIA
SCIENCE FICTION
CARDS FOR CHRISTMAS

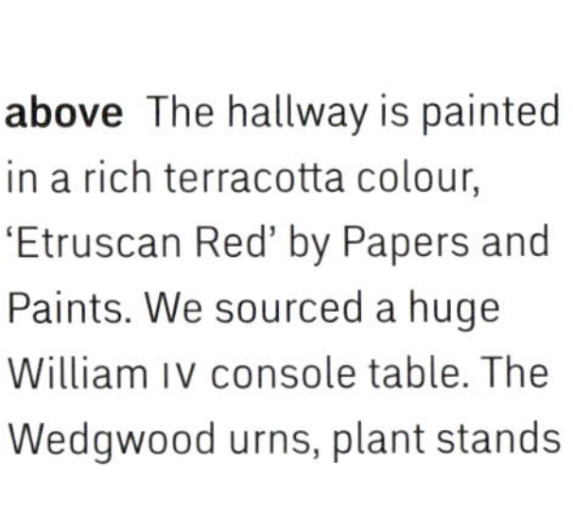

above The hallway is painted in a rich terracotta colour, 'Etruscan Red' by Papers and Paints. We sourced a huge William IV console table. The Wedgwood urns, plant stands and vases were inherited and feel completely at home in this space. Robert Kime's oil lamps are sadly now discontinued.

above The drawing room leads to the library on the principal floor. A vast space with a high ceiling and tall French doors overlooking Gordon Square, the room has evolved through several architectural phases: it has the original white marble fireplaces, but the cornice, frieze and decorative timber screen dividing the two rooms are all early twentieth century. We painted the

background of the frieze in a dark chocolate colour to bring out its delicate pattern and ebonised the screen. The walls are lined in red velvet. This is a room enjoyed in the evening. A nineteenth-century Howard & Sons sofa is upholstered in Robert Kime's 'William Morris Weave', with cushions in one of my favourite patterns, 'Nympheus' by GP & J Baker. A maquette by Nick Hornby is on the right side of the nearest mantelshelf, and the blue vase in the foreground is by Matt Horne.

above Clockwise from top left: a view of the dressing room and into the principal bathroom. The walls are lined in an olive-green linen from Colefax and Fowler. The lampshades are by Melina Blaxland-Horne. The bathroom walls are painted in Farrow & Ball's 'Brinjal', and the bathroom console, with its plaster caryatids, was made for us by Peter Hone.

opposite The principal bedroom is lined in olive-green fabric with a trim in turquoise blue. The lamp is from Westenholz with a marbled shade from Pentreath & Hall. The walls are hung with part of the collection of early photographs; these are images of plants by Karl Blossfeldt. We reused our clients' desk, chair and rug – for us, it is always important to incorporate as many existing pieces as possible into our work.

A Creative Factory

ISLINGTON, LONDON, 2013

Tucked away in a hidden corner of Islington, in north London, accessed down a tiny alleyway, is one of the most unusual of our studio projects, an entirely new house for a close friend of mine, built on the site of an old and derelict Victorian warehouse.

We started by wondering if we could keep the building and restore it, but it was just too far gone. There were cracks so wide you could fit your arm through them, no proper foundations to speak of and a disintegrating roof; the structural engineers ultimately made the decision for us. We were working in the backlands of an old Regency terrace, and we realised that if we respected the volume of the existing building, but changed the forms within, we could create an astonishing new interior. We obtained approval to burrow down, and used slivers of glazing to bring brilliant shafts of light deep into the basement of the house; it feels a bit like being in a Piranesian catacomb.

The brief from my friend was to make a building that looked and felt as if it had been there forever, and we had fun studying the tiniest particulars of Victorian brick warehouse detailing. There is a simple rhythm to the walls and window openings, and the doors and windows are made from rusted metal with deep brick reveals (and note the curved bricks on each corner). There is a depth and solidity to the property that were an important requirement. So much new building – be it contemporary or classical – feels somehow a little ... thin. This was anathema to my friend, who has one of the most remarkable, creative minds. It was our task to create for him a house of ages.

Inside is a classical, elemental structure. We produced a grid of columns and beams running from the basement to the upper floors, cast in concrete that was then shot-blasted to reveal a textural mix of aggregate within. You feel as if you are touching something ancient and powerful, and you cannot help but stroke these walls. The interior is a bold collaboration between our very simple architecture, the creative energy of our client and the textures lent to the building by the unerring eye of Maria Speake, of the London reclamation warehouse Retrouvius, whose philosophy is the innovative reuse of materials. The house, with its combination of old and new, light and dark, small spaces and large volumes, straight lines and curves, has a feeling of rightness and the unexpected in equal measure. It is completely hidden away, revealing itself only to those who enter its magical portal to an imagined past and a creative future.

opposite A tiny passage lined with plants leads into the courtyard garden of this house. The building is entirely new, but we studied Victorian warehouse architecture very carefully in detailing the brickwork, with a dentil cornice and deep curved brick reveals. Huge doors open into the kitchen and hallway, so that the whole house can merge with the outside space in the summer.

following pages The hallway and staircase. A robust concrete frame contains a floating timber-and-metal staircase. Ventilation and mechanical ducting is left exposed, and a bright blue cabinet houses a lift. The floors are in reclaimed timber sourced by Maria Speake of Retrouvius.

previous pages The thrilling kitchen space, with reclaimed boards on the floor and ceiling; a huge, glazed cabinet sourced by Speake; and a stainless-steel kitchen by Alpes Inox. A mirrored backsplash reflects the glazed wall to the courtyard garden behind. It is hard to believe that this building is completely new.

opposite Above, the sitting area adjacent to the open-plan kitchen, with a pair of vintage sofas. The walls are in painted concrete block. To the left, a skylight brings natural light into the back of the house and to the basement floor. Below, a view from the upper-floor mezzanine looking down over the 'great' room at the heart of the house: a sitting, writing and reading room. A vaulted ceiling extends all the way into the roof space.

right A detail of the same room with a vintage glass-fronted museum cabinet filled with model boats built by our clients' son.

Piano / Forte

REGENT'S PARK, LONDON, 2018

Regent's Park again: a glamorous apartment in splendid York Terrace, flooded with light, with the tallest ceilings and four huge *piano nobile* windows facing over the park, and a classical, continental quality to the interior.

Like the townhouse in Chester Terrace, which we saw on pages 48–59, this building had been heavily bombed during the Second World War. Here, little more than the façade was retained, and buildings that had been terraced townhouses were turned into a complex of apartments stretching across the façade. To the rear, Nottingham Terrace was rebuilt in a modish 1960s modernism, which must have felt very fashionable when it was first done. It had experienced fifty years of feeling shabby and unloved, and now strangely feels cool again. The effect of the apartment's surroundings on its interior is interesting: leafy park to the north, 1960s London to the south. I love it.

Our client was the young and fascinating Elisabeth Krohn, who found the studio purely because she walked past the Pentreath & Hall shop in Bloomsbury every week. Intrigued by Bridie's and my ever-changing window displays, she got in touch and asked me to have a look at her new flat. It was a curious place. The previous owners, who had been there for several decades, had commissioned a knowledgeable architect of the old school to completely remodel the interior in the late 1980s in a heavy Louis XVI style. It was put together like a jigsaw puzzle, where if you took away one small element there was a danger the whole thing would unravel.

Elisabeth is Norwegian, and once the rooms were empty of their heavy gilt furniture, there was something of the Nordic soul about them with their tall ceilings and cool north-facing light. We made a decision to keep the panelling in the spacious drawing room and in the dark entrance hall, and to completely remodel the bedroom, bathroom and kitchen.

Harry Pelly was then the decorator in our studio, and he, Elisabeth and I bounced around ideas that fizzed with excitement. The pièce de résistance is the faux-malachite hall, painstakingly created *in situ* by Mathew Bray and Matthew Collins. This space is like a grand symphonic chord followed by moments of stillness and calm: piano-forte on the *piano nobile*. Of all our city projects it is one of my favourites, at once classical and contemporary, filled with Elisabeth's wonderful collection of furniture and objects, magnificent and humble, unexpected and personal, in the best way of all.

opposite Breathtaking faux-malachite decoration on the panelled walls of the hallway, created over many hours of intense labour by the hands of decorative artists Bray and Collins. An eighteenth-century painted cobweb chair and a marquetry console table gleam against this powerful background.

following pages Tall windows face north over Regent's Park; soft light infuses this apartment with a lucid, Scandinavian quality, quite appropriate for our client Elisabeth, who is Norwegian. The panelling is original, and we decided to retain it. The sofa is from Howard & Sons, and the carpet is from Luke Irwin. The furniture is Elisabeth's own or was sourced together with her for the room. We found and installed an antique French eighteenth-century mantelshelf and over mirror.

TASCHEN

A FRAME FOR LIFE
JOHN DERIAN

previous pages Left: a view of the hallway, painted in exuberant faux malachite towards the drawing room. We sourced the eighteenth-century console table and cobweb chairs. Right: four glimpses of two bedrooms and a bathroom, clockwise from top left: the principal bedroom is lined in 'Rose and Fern' hand-blocked chintz by Jean Monro; Elisabeth's parrot sconces hang over the tub in the newly made bathroom; the guest bedroom is lined in the stripy 'Rayure Fleurie' by Madeleine Castaing; and the bathroom panelling is painted in Sanderson's 'Mistflower'.

above and opposite We designed this new kitchen with stripped-back panelling and detailing; a fine Carrara marble backsplash and shelf; and walls painted in 'Mistflower', a pale lilac by Sanderson. The 'Josephine' chairs are by Gavin Houghton. It is a perfect city kitchen.

THE IDEAL COOKERY BOOK
FLYING CULINARY CIRCUS
Nigel Slater
A KITCHEN IN FRANCE
FILIPPO BERIO
OLIO EXTRA VERGINE DI OLIVA

THE ROSE & THISTLE

CHAPTER THREE

TOWNS & TOWNHOUSES

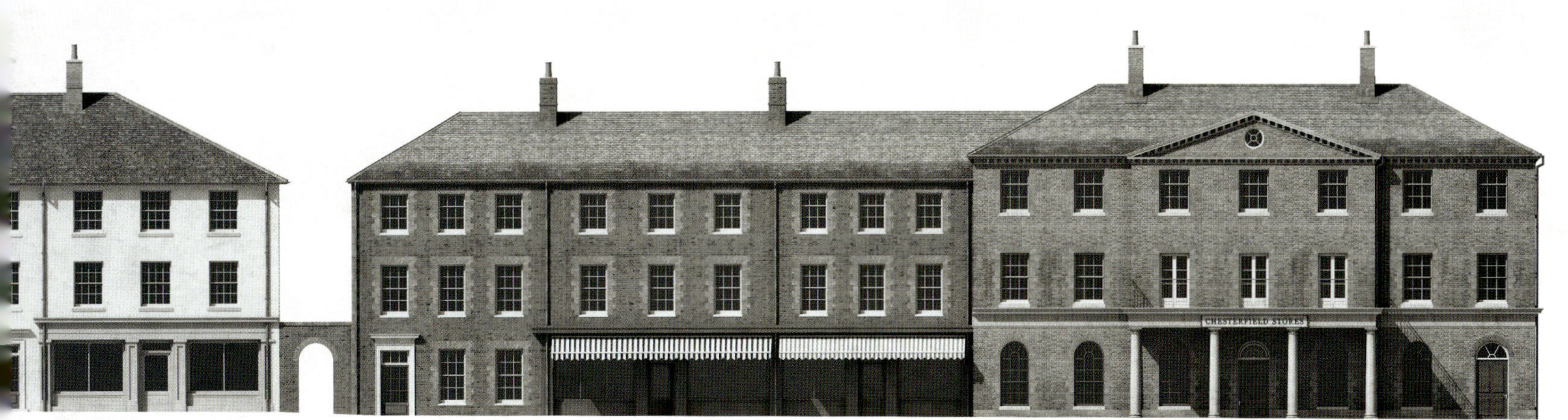

CHAPTER THREE

TOWNS & TOWNHOUSES

I'm building a town. It's a wonderful thing to be able to write. Of course, it's a task of many hands: *we* are building a town. And , as I write on the following pages, the new town of Tornagrain, which the practice is designing and master planning in the Highlands of Scotland, is the project that makes me happiest of all. Perhaps there is something pleasing about white Scottish harling and colourful window frames and doors, and simple architecture, forming streets set against a green and wooded agricultural landscape? Perhaps it's the fact that we are building a frame in which the pictures of people's lives will be lived; or the fact that already it seems to be a happy and well-loved place, when so much new housing is disliked so profoundly. But every now and again there are projects where the alchemy of the ingredients – from site to material to the inspiration of the landowner – renders something where the whole truly feels greater than the sum of its parts.

previous pages A view of Chesterfield Square that we have designed for Welborne, Hampshire: a new town of some six thousand houses that we are master planning and designing for Southwick Estate. The buildings are intended to evoke the character of local towns and villages and will contain a mix of shops, cafés, restaurants and a pub, together with flats and offices. Construction of the town commenced in 2023.

This question of town-building is one that I feel so fortunate to have become involved with. It almost happened by accident. When I left New York I was lucky enough to find a job with the Prince's Foundation for the Built Environment, which had just moved to a fine, converted warehouse in Shoreditch, east London. Here I worked alongside someone who's become a great friend, inspiration and collaborator, Ben Bolgar. We both in turn worked with the brilliant, challenging, thought-provoking urbanist Paul Murrain, who taught me more than I can imagine. Paul introduced me to Andrés Duany, one half of the Florida-based practice Duany Plater-Zyberk, who designed the strategic masterplan for Tornagrain and which we are now executing in detail. Through the Foundation and the Duchy of Cornwall, I was introduced to Léon Krier, the master planner of Poundbury and so much besides, who has become a close friend and mentor. Everything I have learnt started in this place – and honestly, I'm standing on the shoulders of my heros.

With Kim Wilkie, the landscape architect, who I am also lucky enough to count as a close friend, our office is taking forward the masterplan for the Duchy of Cornwall's next great town extension, to the south-east of Faversham, in Kent, which builds on the lessons of the earlier developments and layers in profound strands of landscape, topography, water, green and wooded networks, food production, and circular cycles of water waste and reuse and sustainable energy production.

Increasingly, we realise that architecture is the least important element in all this, and the one that will change most over time (see 'A Sense of Time' on page 32). There are so many more profound ingredients – get those wrong, and no amount of icing on the cake will fix things. But the buildings are what we all notice, and which we live in. Architecture shouldn't be the star of the show, but it's also the thing that makes or breaks how we feel about somewhere. Get the buildings right, and everything feels right. Get them wrong, and everything feels wrong – even if all the underlying factors are well placed.

There are a few lessons that I have learnt in all this:

The power of repetition: if you design a beautiful house, the more you build, the more beautiful a place can become. We need some variety to keep things interesting, but less than you'd think: look at the streets of eighteenth-century Bath, Liverpool or London. The twentieth century, which made a habit of constructing countless horrible building types again and again, has given this idea a bad name. It's time to reclaim the basic beauty of elegant repetition in our streets and towns.

Simplicity is the prevailing virtue in urbanism: the rich architectural flourish has its moment, but providing the 'good ordinary' background is truly the task of our great urban streets.

The best lessons for any new placemaking are generally to be found within a fifteen-mile radius of the site: you can travel the world looking at examples, but the most useful are often right in front of your eyes. Search carefully for them, and don't be afraid of copying the best and most successful. It is how to make new places belong where they are.

Our work in towns is not merely with new building. Sometimes, we're stitching new streets into old places – as in our work in the ancient cities of Chichester or Truro – and very often we're working on wonderful, individual old buildings in Victorian or Edwardian streets – as with many of the projects illustrated in these pages. These encompass some of my favourite things: combining everything I love in one single essence – urbane, civilised, dignified architecture; the satisfaction of gentle restoration and careful repair; and the final magical ingredient, the narrative of the fantastic atmosphere of decoration. The full scale of our studio's work, from quartet to symphony, can be found here, just like turning the dial of the radio. I love the different tunes you catch, as much as the static in between.

A New Town for the Highlands

TORNAGRAIN, SCOTLAND, 2010–

Are we allowed favourite projects? This new town in the Scottish Highlands, which will be more than a lifetime in the making, may have to qualify, for it's here that so much that I am interested in has aligned.

Tornagrain is the conception of my wonderful client the 21st Earl of Moray, who kindly wrote the foreword to this book. Almost twenty-five years ago, John was approached by the Highland Council to discuss emerging plans for a series of satellite commuter 'villages' to the east of Inverness. The capital city of the Scottish Highlands was suffering from decades of ill-thought-out expansion and suburban sprawl, and the council was trying to plan more carefully for the decades of growth to come.

John understood its intention but was worried that this beautiful landscape of his childhood, the Moray Firth, was itself in danger of becoming suburbanised, as none of the settlements being considered had the scale or structure to become a self-supporting town. He and his estate manager Andrew Howard embarked on a tour of all the best-practice new developments in Britain, Europe and beyond. It was this journey that led them to Andrés Duany, the world-renowned master planner and head of Florida-based practice DPZ. Andrés and his team were commissioned to consider an alternative proposal for a single town. The design workshop was held on-site in the autumn of 2006, and I was one of a number of architects and designers involved in the conceptualisation of the new vision. That's where I first met John and his wife Cathy, who have steered this amazing project through ever since.

We were commissioned to take forward the execution of Tornagrain, which broke ground in 2015. By the summer of 2023, the first three hundred houses were occupied. One day the town will contain up to five thousand homes, one secondary and two primary schools, employment spaces, health centres and a new high street, which we are planning in detail as I write. A central park occupies the heart of the town, and there is a wide network of allotments and outdoor space, and thousands of trees are being planted.

The architectural language draws carefully from the local vernacular, but there is a special extra dimension here. Houses in the Highlands are inexpensive, and we must therefore keep construction costs as low as possible. This has meant that there are few embellishments. The whole place is intentionally simple; landscape and built form do the work. Tornagrain, as a result, feels immensely settled in its place. As I often say, new developments *can* be beautiful and, with care, they need not cost the earth.

opposite The first phase of Tornagrain, with the curve of Croy Road in the foreground. A mix of houses, cottages, shops and apartments lines the streets and square, with parking neatly tucked in behind the buildings, in parking courts and in the ground-floor garages of mews flats. The local palette of traditional rendered walls is enlivened with splashes of colour from corrugated iron roofs and painted timber buildings. Close by is an existing clump of mature trees that forms the centre of the new town park; beyond that will be future phases of the town, including the new high street and town square. In the distance are the Moray Firth and the Black Isle.

following pages Tornagrain at sunset, with a view over houses and rooftops to the Black Isle. The cottages follow the line of the existing Croy Road, its sinuous S-shaped curve creating an alluring sense of flow through the new houses. All over Tornagrain are streets that you can't wait to explore and discover what is just around the corner. In the foreground are woods and a path leading to the open countryside, which surrounds the new town.

TÒRR NA GRÈINE

LOCHANDINT
LANE
PHARMACY

above Croy Square is at the heart of the initial phase of Tornagrain. Here, three-storey buildings line the square to create a sense of enclosure at this first of many local centres that we will design for the various neighbourhoods of the town. Red detailing on the tall apartment block brings a welcome dose of colour to the street scene.

opposite We never quite anticipated the pleasing sense of curves in two directions, around the corner and down the hill, until construction started on this terrace. A successful village shop and local pharmacy bring a feeling of energy to this first phase of the town. Traffic passing to and from neighbouring villages has helped these pioneer businesses trade with positive results.

following pages Tornagrain has a strong landscape character, with a huge variety of green spaces. Larger green expanses are lined with townhouses – a pathway is tucked between two garden rooms; more intimate spaces are fronted by small cottages, as here at Malvina Green. A broad greenway runs through the town because of an existing oil pipeline route, necessity being the mother of invention. The whole town is surrounded by richly wooded rolling hills (pages 102–3).

GY65 CCE

A Happy Home for a Young Family

WANDSWORTH, LONDON, 2018

Skye McAlpine and her husband Anthony are close friends of Charlie's and mine. Skye is a brilliant cook and writer, with a large and loyal following on social media, and as a result her butter-yellow kitchen is, I would imagine, better known than any other we've designed.

Skye approached us with a degree of trepidation when she and Anthony bought this house, in a tall, generously proportioned Victorian building in Wandsworth, but which had been brutally converted in the late 1980s, complete with terrible joinery, uPVC windows and plastic floors. Would I be able to help them on a limited budget and, also, with a new baby on the way, in the very short amount of time before they needed to move?

There's no job too small in our studio, so long as the project is interesting and the people are lovely. We've recently, for instance, done a single room in a beautiful house in Bloomsbury. It's not all about huge houses with massive budgets – in fact, the smaller undertakings can be the most rewarding projects of all. So, we had a wonderful time taking on this unloved old house and making it into one of the happiest, sunniest, friendliest homes that you've ever seen. Skye and Anthony's sense of generosity fills and infuses each room. Nothing is too serious here.

The house was unlisted, and none of the interior was original, so we had the untrammelled joy of knocking through walls and hacking around with abandon, before putting back cornices and floors and architectural detail. On the ground floor, Skye wanted a spacious kitchen and long table for her famous supper parties. Upstairs, we created a handsome, light-filled drawing room overlooking Wandsworth Common, and a study; the bedroom floor came next, where we did the opposite of what most people would do and made a large bathroom at the front of the house and a quieter, small cocoon of a bedroom at the back. The children are upstairs in the best attic bedrooms of all, with views over the Common in one direction and London rooftops in the other.

The house was finished by skilful young builders in record time, and Skye and Anthony moved in just before their baby arrived. There was never a harsh word spoken or a problem unsolved, proving, as always in life, that you get out of it exactly what you put in. It's a worthy lesson in architecture and design, and I think you can tell as much from these pages.

opposite Paintings by young children, for me, are as special as anything by a famous contemporary artist. Here, in Skye and Anthony's son's room, framed pictures and a little Australian flag are vibrant against green 'Jardin' wallpaper by Antoinette Poisson, Paris. We found the green-and-white neo-Regency fire surround.

above A cook's dream: Skye's kitchen is hardworking and practical, with a wide steel Lacanche range. The cabinets are painted in two shades – butter and buttercup yellow – partly inspired by Claude Monet's kitchen and dining room at Giverny. The island, an old kitchen table we found (and to which we added a marble top), is on sturdy wheels so that it can be pushed out into the garden when Skye needs a long table for one of her renowned supper parties.

opposite A yellow Smeg fridge provides a cheerful note, and enamelled cans below an old table function as wastebins. We sourced old potters' boards to create the shelving along this wall. A Pentreath & Hall creamware lidded vase – a birthday present from Charlie and me – sits atop the fridge.

following pages The walls of the kitchen and adjacent dining area are finished in an Italian plaster. Skye and Anthony found the tall glazed cupboard housing china and glass on a shopping trip to Brussels. We painted it pale grey and added a lining paper by Antoinette Poisson. A pair of candy-coloured striped curtains completes the scene.

SMEG
BREAD

left Skye's study on the first floor is painted in a gloss lipstick red. We originally designed this double-sided ottoman for the main bathroom, but it has migrated downstairs and feels completely at home among the books. I have a personal rule never to arrange book spines by colour, but Skye is very organised and it suits her well. When I was taking these photographs, I noticed that she also arranges her phone apps by colour, so I will let her off. The drawing room can be glimpsed through the doorway.

opposite The first-floor drawing room has high ceilings and tall windows looking straight over leafy Wandsworth Common. We washed the walls in a soft pink; the fireplace is antique nineteenth-century French, and the deep sofa from George Sherlock is upholstered in the hand-blocked 'Rose and Fern' chintz from Jean Monro. The bar fridge to the left is vintage Fornasetti.

following pages Skye and Anthony's bedroom is lined in a now-discontinued Warner Fabrics textile that Harry Pelly, the project decorator, found on Radio H-P. It's the most romantic room. An antique steel four-poster bed is filled with comfortable pillows, and an air of glamour comes from the lacquered Edwardian cabinet desk with its glossy cherry-red interior.

IRIS ORIGO

Arts & Crafts Restored

HAMPSTEAD, LONDON, 2013

Just off leafy Frognal, a famous Hampstead street, was a fine but exhausted Edwardian house: unlisted, oak stained black, claret-red carpets throughout. We saw through the gloom, and mapped out a vision over pints of beer that evening in The Holly Bush pub. So began this adventure.

Our clients wanted to infuse a sense of light and space into this old building with its little inglenooks and low beams, to create a feeling of warmth and generosity in place of claustrophobia. The house had excellent bones and was sitting in a sizeable secret garden. We worked with local architect Chris Pask, always a pleasure to collaborate with, bringing his passion for Edwin Lutyens and the best of the Arts and Crafts Movement to this task. Chris handled a not uncomplicated planning situation and looked after the restoration of the building; we oversaw the architectural interiors, furnishings and decoration.

Rooms were opened up, panelling restored and installed, oakwork stripped and refinished. The building was restored for the first time in generations, reroofed and windows rebuilt or repaired. It was a huge task, made more complex still by the creation of a basement and the construction of a bright, sunny new kitchen wing facing the garden to the west, complete with a double-height, top-lit dome, loosely inspired by Lutyens's work at Castle Drogo.

We embarked on the decoration together with our clients, creating a shared vision that draws on the best of the Arts and Crafts Movement, with fine Edwardian furniture, but never dusty and dry: a house that brings colour, pattern and modernity to its flow. Josef Frank fabrics sit alongside those from Morris & Co.; dark-coloured grasscloth alongside more delicate patterns and prints. The owners have built up a wonderful and expanding collection of mid-twentieth-century pictures including an enviable number of works by Edward Bawden, whose linocuts and watercolours are suddenly now rather rare. The house has evolved too, with new bedrooms being made for more children, and the sitting room you see here recently being painted a bright custard yellow and becoming a games room. It's a lovely shift as the family grows larger and older. The best projects are never caught in aspic. Houses are 'a frame for life', as the brilliant and inspirational designer Ilse Crawford so aptly put it, and the frame changes as life unfolds.

As I write, we are starting work on a marvellous new house for this happy family in the Peak District, also an Arts and Crafts design, but with a high Victorian ring to it, from the hand of esteemed architect William Eden Nesfield. The adventure continues and gets only more interesting as life moves on: just how I like it.

opposite We stripped the heavy dark-stained oak of the original staircase, and after a heroic effort it was refinished in this much warmer and lighter limed-oak stain. Charlie and I found the collection of original nineteenth-century pressed ferns at Portobello Road Market early one morning; they look as if they have always been here. I papered the stairs in a Morris & Co. wallpaper, 'Marigold', in the muted Linen colourway. The 'Letchworth' lantern is from Jamb.

above The oak staircase is original to the house. The panelling, too, is old, but after some attempts at lightening it, we painted it in Farrow & Ball's 'Old White', with a dead-flat finish. We found an Arts and Crafts hanging lamp and oak table for the hallway, and the floors throughout this part of the house are carpeted in rush matting from the esteemed Felicity Irons.

opposite This comfortable sitting room is lined in a small geometric print fabric (now sadly discontinued), with painted panelling beyond to match the original. The sofa is from B&B Italia and the deep armchairs from George Sherlock, the far one upholstered in 'Nympheus' fabric by GP & J Baker. The carpet is from Luke Irwin.

BRITAIN
in AUTUMN

opposite and above Architect Chris Pask and I conceived the double-height kitchen, loosely inspired by Lutyens's design at Castle Drogo. The cabinetry is to our standard design, and I found the antique Edwardian glazed dresser on eBay for a few hundred pounds (although we had to spend rather more to refinish the heavily stained wood). The fabric of the curtains in the foreground opposite is an absolute favourite, Josef Frank's 'Rox & Fix' by Svenskt Tenn. The ebonised chairs were made for us by Lawrence Neal, to designs now available from Marchmont Workshop.

following pages A luxurious principal bedroom is finished in a dark olive-green grasscloth, with Morris & Co. 'Marigold' curtains and bed fabric by Veere Grenney. The desk conceals an end-of-bed television, made to our design by Rupert Bevan. In the attic (pages 122–3), we knocked together three tiny and awkward 'maids bedrooms' to form a new oak-panelled sitting room, with deep, comfortable sofas and a huge squashy ottoman to my own design. The striped dhurrie is by Guinevere Antiques, and the suzani cushion on the armchair is from Pentreath & Hall.

The Eclectic Cottage

ISLINGTON, LONDON, 2016

This is Bridie's home: Bridie, who is such a remarkable half of my working and creative life, the 'Hall' in Pentreath & Hall. When she took on this beautiful three-and-a-half-storey cottage in Victorian-brick Islington, she had the clearest vision of things, but of course we came together to help.

Bridie and I met almost twenty years ago. I wasn't long back from New York. She'd been house-painting a beautiful Regency residence for mutual friends, and it was at homeowner Thomas's birthday party that I spied a present on his mantelshelf: a hand-cast, blackened and waxed plaster column base. 'Who made this?' I asked. 'It's amazing'. And so, I was introduced to Bridie, thanks to that little piece of plaster sitting on a shelf. Fifteen years ago, we opened Pentreath & Hall together, which is really a different story from either this house or this book, but the warp and weft of our lives are so closely intertwined that it's hard to know where one strand of the thread ends and another starts. Every day working with Bridie has been a pleasure, and it only gets better.

Bridie's house is not actually tiny, but it has that *feel* about it that makes you want to call it so. One of my favourite things about it is the slender original stairway that leads to a tucked-away attic bathroom. There is Bridie's bedroom and dressing room, with new French doors and staircase out to a roof terrace, planted with a flourishing jungle, home to a family of mice. Below is the main sitting room, filled with treasures, like a museum, and Bridie's austere workroom next door. And below, maybe the heart of this home, her sitting–dining room and kitchen, with a bold white-and-red floor, home to tortoises Sir David (Attenborough) and Mayhem, and Albie the cat. Max, Bridie's poodle, is rather a distinguished old man now, a famous part of the Pentreath & Hall story.

But the question really is: is this the first book on decorating you've seen with a photograph showing a tortoise on the kitchen floor? This room is the scene of many a day and night when Bridie and I have plotted ideas for the year to come; or years, I should say, because nothing in the world of shops or making things gets done very fast, at least if you want to do it well, like we do. Luckily, the house moved a little more quickly. She chased the builders out, literally, as the removals van was arriving, and then the Wunderkammer began.

opposite Bridie's beautiful four-poster bed was designed and made for her by Marianna Kennedy, who also makes the resin lamps with book-cloth lampshades that are a true staple of our decoration work – here, in clear and dreamy pale lilac. Bridie designed the bedside table as a prototype that one day we might bring into production. The shelves are filled with her collection of plaster Platonic solids and other delights. Two beautiful Egyptian textiles hang above the bed.

following pages Bridie's narrow entrance hall is densely arranged with a collection of Peter Hone plaster casts, an homage both to our great friend and collaborator who designed them and to the installation at Sir John Soane's Museum. Bridie installed the timber wainscotting and painted it gloss brown. We designed the shelves for Bridie's sitting room, which has become an astonishing cabinet of curiosities. The chair in the foreground was designed by Bridie, and the framed picture beneath the shelves was painted by Glenn Brown.

LINDSEY HILSUM IN EXTREMIS MARIE COLVIN
MINIMALISMO
INSPIRATION

opposite Corners of Bridie's house, clockwise from top left: the view from the kitchen into the dining room, with a cheerful red-and-white checked lino floor; the attic stairway, with leopard-print carpet; the olive-green kitchen, with open shelves painted in Farrow & Ball's 'India Yellow', and plain white six-inch-square tiles; and a pink bathroom with cork tiles on the floor.

above A detail of Bridie's pantry with part of her collection of china.

following pages Bridie's dining room is a wonderfully happy space, scene of many parties. Daffodils from her garden brighten the day. The green cabinet and lamp are by Bridie Hall, the print above is by Robyn Denny, the fireplace was marbled by Ian Harper, and the gloss red floor is home to Sir David, the tortoise, who you can just glimpse between the chair legs. The creamware candlestick and Eric Ravilious print above the fireplace are from Pentreath & Hall.

Cool and Airy in Leafy Chelsea

CHELSEA, LONDON, 2012

'Will you come and help me with a corner of old Chelsea?' was the request that arrived in the office years ago, when we were a much smaller studio. This was one of our first private house commissions in London, restoring a handsome old artist's studio tucked away off the King's Road.

The house, like so many we see, was in one sense perfect, with the layers and accretions of time that you can never make up. It had been lived in for decades by an artist, who still used the spacious, north-facing, double-height room as her painting studio. Her library was filled with an enviable collection of books; the kitchen, tucked in a lean-to extension at the side of the house, was like stepping into nineteenth-century France, with a butter-yellow stove and blue-and-white tiles on the walls. But the house was almost collapsing. The roof was broken, windows were hanging off their hinges, and the extensions were falling away from the main house. Parts of the building had been split into separate flats with tiny bathrooms, each with an ancient immersion heater. It was time, I was sad to say, for a deep restoration.

We were asked to create several new bedrooms, family rooms and a large, open kitchen that connected to the garden, and to bring a sense of light and space to the whole. Our client has a gentle, almost enigmatic, sensibility that reminds me of the quiet heroines of E.M. Forster novels. Her life is busier than many, but in the middle of it all she has a sense of calm that exudes throughout the house. She has an unerring eye for fine pictures and objects, and made excellent choices for the key walls and locations in each room.

In the first-floor studio, we created a family sitting room, with generous sofas and a large TV for watching films, and a new oak-framed window in place of the decaying old one. We uncovered the tiny old fireplace with its original emerald-green tiles. From a ground-floor sitting room, we formed a new family kitchen that leads to a conservatory beyond. More bedrooms and bathrooms were created in the attic and side wing.

This is an ordinary Victorian 1840s brick house, made extraordinary by two things: its garden and the late nineteenth-century studio. Both now play leading roles again. Today, the garden gate swings open frequently to a revolving band of the family's daughters and their many friends. It is a house filled with people and laughter, but with a serenity at its core.

opposite The original nineteenth-century artist's studio has very high ceilings and a tall, north-facing window that we completely rebuilt. The room is painted in the palest warm grey, a gentle background to a collection of mid-twentieth-century British art. The chair from George Sherlock is upholstered in a yellow linen; beside it is a rattan table by Soane Britain. The window-seat cushion is by Guy Goodfellow.

following pages Looking the other way, a set of old metal shelves sourced from Retrouvius houses a lovely collection of art books; a deeply comfortable 'Wardour Sofa' by Jasper Conran is the nicest place to sit and read them all. The palette in this room is calm and gentle, just like our client. The fine Ivon Hitchens landscape above the books provides just the right splash of colour.

A LIFE OF PICASSO
Rubens in Private
Rembrandt
Essential CONSTABLE
HENRI MATISSE
MARC CHAGALL
CEZANNE by himself
John Rewald CEZANNE
Perfect lighting

art
HOWARD HODGKIN PAINTINGS
Francis Bacon
FRANCIS BACON
Frank Auerbach
LUCIAN FREUD
PICASSO
THE SHOCK OF THE NEW
Henry Moore
Ivon Hitchens
CHADWICK
SUTHERLAND
THE CRUSADES
PALMER
Victor Pasmore
COLLECTIBLES
Writers on Howard Hodgkin
BEN NICHOLSON

opposite and above The dining conservatory, which we added to the house, and the new kitchen illustrate the simplicity in form and colour that we used in the design. The table from Bulthaup and pale floors in Dinesen oak contrast with the dark green joinery and the richly coloured 'Aralia' fabric designed by Josef Frank for Svenskt Tenn. This room is really all about the view to the leafy garden beyond.

above Clockwise from top left: the principal bedroom and dressing room are gentle and restrained; in the attic is a wallpaper by Marthe Armitage; and the arched window in the twin bedroom tells a story – it was from here that the Suffragette campaigner Emmeline Pankhurst gave a rousing speech to a crowd of supporters in the street below, before being arrested and sent to prison.

opposite We designed an austere principal bathroom in Carrara and pale Bardiglio marbles. The Wyatt chair (and its matching pair in the bedroom) was bought from the Duchess of Devonshire's sale at Sotheby's in 2016.

following pages A view from the attic bedroom down to the leafy garden, one of the most special things about this lovely Victorian house: a quiet oasis in the heart of 'old Chelsea'.

A Town for the King

POUNDBURY, DORCHESTER, DORSET, 2001–

On a hill in West Dorset is one of the most famous examples of new urban thinking in Europe – a shining beacon for architecture today. Poundbury needs little introduction to most: this is King Charles III's new town, his urban extension to Dorchester. We have worked here for two decades.

The plan was conceived when King Charles was a young Prince of Wales, on land owned by his great estate, the Duchy of Cornwall (see also 'A New Crescent for a Small City' on pages 60–5). The Duchy has existed since the fourteenth century to provide independence to the heir to the throne. King Charles was the 24th Duke of Cornwall, and Poundbury is the foremost of his architectural legacies, the physical embodiment of much of his nascent thinking about architecture that began with his broadcast of 1988, and the V&A exhibition and book of the same title, *A Vision of Britain*, a year later.

Léon Krier is the master planner of Poundbury, bringing this idea to reality. The plan turns conventional, post-war suburban sprawl on its head: the town is laid out with a network of gently curving streets, in a series of connected, walkable neighbourhoods. A wide variety of houses sits adjacent to shops, cafés and commercial spaces, and at the middle of the settlement is the central Queen Mother Square. There is a large school and health centre overlooking a new urban park, plenty of allotments and green squares, and a regular bus service into the centre of Dorchester. It would be completely possible to live and work today in Poundbury without a car: what a radical proposition that is, if you think about the long arc of post-war suburban expansion, and how we have planned out our world.

At the instigation of His Royal Highness, 35 per cent of Poundbury's homes are built to provide affordable and social accommodation, seamlessly designed into each street scene rather than being hidden away in one corner (or, still worse, banished from the development entirely, which was completely the norm when Poundbury started).

For twenty years I have been designing houses in Poundbury, and I suppose the studio has been responsible for more than 1,500 buildings here now. What an astonishing privilege, and a lesson learnt, which I try to take elsewhere. For decades, Poundbury was derided by critics as 'pastiche' and backward-looking. The Prince of Wales received a huge amount of criticism from the sidelines, as this vision for a different way of building was ridiculed by commentators and architects alike. Today, it feels as if his powerfully prescient philosophy has been vindicated. Poundbury, and the Duchy's new developments at Nansledan, in Cornwall, and even more recently at Faversham, in Kent (which I am master planning with Kim Wilkie), all seem to address the urgent questions of how we house an expanding population, in sympathy with nature and the landscape, by learning from the best examples of history.

opposite The tower of Royal Pavilion in fading evening summer light. Designed to be at the centre of Krier's extraordinary masterplan for Poundbury, Royal Pavilion's six-storey tower soars above the rooftops of the town. The room at the top is effectively an enormous domed lantern, and it has remarkable views across the countryside of west Dorset. I designed it with canted corners so that there would always be one corner sheltered from a breeze. The copper-coloured cupola above the dome is modelled on the Choragic Monument of Lysicrates, built in the fourth century BCE and which still stands in a square in Athens.

above An informal green park sits in the middle of Woodlands Crescent, the first phase of which I designed when I was working with Fairfax & Sammons in New York; the crescent is in the heart of Poundbury. I love the natural desire-line footpath that opens up across the park.

opposite Two views of more recent phases of the town: detached houses on Duke of Edinburgh Garden (top) have a nineteenth-century flavour, with rich architectural embellishment and black-painted window frames; and a corner of the bustling Buttermarket (bottom), lined with shops and a post office, completed in 2016, at the heart of the South West Quadrant.

BUTTERMARKET
Stores
THE

opposite In the heart of the Queen Mother Square district, we have designed two buildings with arcaded brick forms based on Krier's 'palazzina' apartment blocks. The ground floors of both blocks have commercial use with underground parking, allowing the buildings to achieve a very high density of residential units per hectare – a model for civilised and successful urban development.

right The arched base of Royal Pavilion. I designed this building in a Greco-Roman language of restrained Greek Doric trabeated form but with a soaring vaulted arch. The stonework is in reconstructed Portland stone by Haddonstone, all detailed at full size by our office, and beautifully built by C.G. Fry & Son, one of the renowned developers of Poundbury.

following pages Views of different residential corners of Poundbury designed by the studio: a gently curving street in the South West Quadrant (left), with painted-brick paired cottages; painted stucco houses around Hayward Square (right, top and centre), with the terrace on the right designed by Poundbury co-architect George Saumarez Smith; brick houses and a tall stone obelisk (right, bottom), designed by the Ben Pentreath Studio on the southern edge of Poundbury, with deep south-facing ironwork balconies.

KW53 OET

Poundbury during a midsummer sunrise, with the tower of Royal Pavilion soaring above the rooftops. The field of barley in the foreground demonstrates the relationship between Poundbury and the agricultural landscape of west Dorset all around.

CHAPTER FOUR

THE COUNTRY HOUSE

I've drawn houses for as long as I can remember. Science was my least favourite subject when I was young, but it provided good supplies of graph paper, which I covered with rather grand and unexpected designs for palaces. The habit started getting serious by the time I was thirteen. Around then, my parents moved for a few months to my grandparents' old house, on a magical site surrounded by woodland leading down to the Beaulieu River, one of the most beautiful places in the whole of southern England. In the 1950s my grandparents had built for themselves a shingle-clad bungalow on the tightest budget imaginable. It was a wonderful house: all about the connection to landscape and view. Inside it was decorated by my granny with a brilliant combination of old country house furniture (that she had bought at auctions just after the war) and Festival of Britain colours and fabrics. My grandfather's study, filled with treasures – he was an expert on the classical Greek and Roman worlds – was painted a rich burnt-red colour, and memorably the dining room had a bright purple ceiling. The building itself was simple, which is an interesting lesson to us all: increasingly, I'm realising that it's really all about landscape, and how buildings sit *in* the landscape, rather than about the buildings themselves. I'd always loved my grandparents' house but living there added an extra dimension.

previous pages A design for a new country villa in Oxfordshire. We obtained planning consent for this house in 2023, after two and a half years. The design is based on Palladian villas of the Veneto, and references the Menagerie at Horton, the magical house rescued and restored by Gervase Jackson-Stops and Ian Kirby, as well as other English Palladian examples.

For fun, I started imagining what we'd do if we built a new house on this special piece of land near the river. I played with ideas both contemporary and traditional, sketching away in a fantasy land of my own creation.

I'd say it was around that time too that my fascination with old houses was expanding dramatically. Visits to National Trust properties (then at their peak of civilised, informed, educational display under the stewardship of the late Gervase Jackson-Stops as architectural adviser) fuelled my burgeoning interest; back in the school library I devoured books on Georgian houses and buildings. From these I started more painstaking and laborious drawings, designing versions of my own, often with alarmingly thin walls or other structural challenges. My friend the architect George Saumarez Smith has a good observation in life, 'You are as an adult who you were as a child', and when I look at my old drawings, I realise that everything I'm interested in today is something that has been deeply ingrained for a very long time: brick or stonework, panelling, sash windows, proportions. While along the way we absorb thousands of influences – every place we visit (either in person or in photographs, and in the mind) changes our way of thinking and seeing, and like a musician doing scales we become more confident and better with practice – the foundations are there from the start.

I suppose it's no surprise then that so much of our work is in and with the world of the country house, old and new. Partly, this is the natural realm of the traditional architect today, perhaps for obvious reasons. I love working with old houses, and a huge amount of our time is spent on the careful restoration and repair of these buildings, employed either by the historic families who own them, or by people breathing new life into their old bones. It is a happy task. The decoration is possibly the most creative element, drawing together colours, fabrics, furniture and objects, working either with historic collections or helping to build new ones. There is a spirit to these places that does not like being set in aspic: they are living, breathing things, not museums. Houses of great age have the ability to absorb objects and fabrics and colours of all periods. I have been fascinated by the interiors of David Hicks for at least as long as I've been an architect, or the early work of John Fowler, or decorators such as Billy Baldwin in the United States, who understood powerfully the relationship between old buildings and a contemporary sensibility in decoration, at once fascinating and unexpected. These are themes that I found myself returning to again and again in my previous two books, *English Decoration* and *English Houses*. A decade further on, I hope that our own work as a practice holds up (most of the time) to the values of so many of these examples, creating rooms that are at once of today and timeless. I'm not sure I can be the judge of that myself.

A few years ago, I wrote an article for the *Financial Times* that certainly raised some eyebrows when it was published: 'Why do so many horrible people want to build neo-Georgian houses?'. Of course, it was partly tongue-in-cheek, but there was a kernel of truth in what I was saying. I have been so fortunate to work with some kind, happy, funny and often extremely unusual clients. Maybe that article managed to see off the bullies, the hedge-fund managers and the psychopaths who I was referring to, and who really do seem to enjoy commissioning large classical houses. Either way, we have been lucky. There is an act of creation involved in building a new house that is a sign of an immensely positive outlook, of an optimism that I find is increasingly rare and valuable in our world: an approach which chooses not to believe that all problems are insurmountable, and which draws succour and advice from the long lessons of history.

I'll admit, too, that we have struggled as an architectural practice to have some of our new houses built. We have designed many that for various reasons – complications with planners or budgets, or indeed of great personal sadness (a few years ago, for instance, a revered client was taken by cancer shortly before we were due to start the project) – haven't happened. I am sanguine about this because we have had so many wonderful collaborations in these last twenty years, and in a sense the moment of design is the really creative piece, more so than the execution. I love visiting the Sir John Soane's Museum, but there is always a tinge of regret at the number of unbuilt designs for which Soane and his office prepared beautiful drawings. But it is a happy time for me to be writing as, for whatever reason, we have many new projects on-site and in construction drawings, as well as the completed houses which I'm able to show here. As always with architecture, the idea of tomorrow is perhaps more exciting than the reality of today.

A Rare Alignment

SOUTHERN ENGLAND, 2006–

Every designer has a project in life where elements combine in a way that is unexpected, where the whole is greater than the sum of its parts: a perfect alignment of site, energy and the combined vision of architect and owner. These projects don't happen often, maybe once in a lifetime, twice or more if we are lucky.

This, for me, is one such place. I will never forget the call that I took on the first or second day of the year, when I was having a quiet time catching up on things in the office before the New Year rush. 'We've been thinking about making some changes to our house', a friendly voice said on the phone. 'Could I come and see you to talk about it?' A few days later we met at the Goring Hotel, and the conversation felt a good one. I made a plan to see the site and from here began what turned out to be a long journey, one of the happiest of my professional life.

The house is in a fine village and has an interesting history. A former rectory, it had been reworked by the renowned architect Quinlan Terry in the early 1980s. The new owners wished to enlarge the house with a pair of wings, add a swimming pool building, and undertake a general remodelling.

As I began to draw, the bones of a H-shaped house in the late Queen Anne–early Georgian mode began to emerge, with brick walls, hipped roofs and both dormer and tall sash windows. We discussed removing a floor at the front of the house to carve out a double-height entrance hall. New living rooms, kitchens and bedrooms took shape on plan. A few months later, we submitted for planning (a task that has become ever more terrifying, and challenging, over the last twenty years), and amazingly the application breezed through without a murmur, merely with a complimentary letter of support from the conservation and design officer. How hard it might be to find that response today.

We took a long time to start and a long time to build. The office was tiny in those days: me and just one or two others. We had time to draw, to *really* draw. I was ably helped by my first-ever assistant, Luke Bennett, in the initial phase of works, and by the unerring eye of a young Rupert Cunningham in the second. Today, Rupert is the studio's senior design director. It was a wonderful learning journey for us all. Pip Morrison designed the landscape, the first of so many projects we have collaborated on together. And gently, slowly, our remarkable clients have furnished the house, with the lightest-touch help from our decoration studio over the years. From all these ingredients, on what was really my first and still almost my largest private house project, the pieces of the jigsaw puzzle came together: truly, a happy, complete and perfect English vision.

opposite A newly made oak door in the library, beautifully constructed in quarter-sawn oak and hand finished, with ebonised detail, all to full-size designs by the studio.

following pages The west front of the house feels most like my own work because it is the only façade that is not seen in the context of the existing parts of the old house. The walls are in beautiful handmade and wood-fired bricks by Jim Matthews of H.G. Matthews, laid in lime mortar. The roof is clay peg tile. Veteran trees and the astonishing plans of the landscape architect Pip Morrison, as well as the labours of our green-fingered client, give this façade – less than eight years old in this photograph – a wonderful, settled feel.

right This double-height entrance hall is a completely new room. We carved the space out of two floors of the old central portion of the house. The lower walls are panelled, with fluted Doric columns and deep, hand-carved brackets to my drawings, holding up the timber gallery. The walls above are in plaster. Through an arched doorway is the new oak staircase we designed (see page 163). The floor is in English limestone, and we designed the pair of bolection fireplaces in carved marble. The giltwood chandeliers are to a design by William Kent.

opposite Clockwise from top left: the west attic stair is in a robust painted timber design; the east wing staircase is in stone with metal balusters from ground to first floor, and timber (to the same design) from first to attic; the first-floor landing; ground-floor detailing of the main oak staircase shown on the page opposite. A low arch leads to the garden door.

right The main staircase is in hand-carved English oak and is based closely on early eighteenth-century examples, especially from a fine demolished house in Great Ormond Street (a stone's throw from the studio). Beautiful measured drawings of that staircase were taken in the 1930s, which formed the basis of our design here. The ceiling is in plasterwork by the talented Geoffrey Preston, inspired by a number of precedents including Mompesson House in Salisbury Cathedral Close, Wiltshire.

Bread

previous pages A fine eighteenth-century chimneypiece in the drawing room is from Jamb. Here we see a corner of the same room, which is in a completely new wing, with windows and shutters to our details and a plaster cornice from the Stevensons of Norwich 'National Trust' range, which I designed. The campaign sofa in the centre of the photograph was bought from Edward Hurst, dealer extraordinaire. It is now covered in a Fortuny silk.

opposite A corner of the new kitchen to our design, with a Yorkstone flagged floor and a range surround in Bath stone. The countertops are in Mandale Fossil stone from Derbyshire, a beautiful grey stone that we use often. The room is made special by our clients' collection of old apothecary jars. The lights are from Christopher Howe.

above The breakfast and sitting room has a deep sofa and a Bath stone bolection fire surround to the generous woodburning stove. The door leads to utility rooms, and beyond to the swimming pool building shown on page 173.

previous pages The principal bedroom is in the new wing, facing south-west. The wallpaper is by de Gournay, specially coloured and aged for the house. The chimneypiece was originally in the old drawing room and relocated here. The bed, in a Chinese style, was commissioned by my client.

above The dressing room is in one of the original parts of the house, but with panelling installed in the 1980s to designs by the distinguished classical architect Kit Rae-Scott. The room was beautifully designed, and we made no changes.

opposite Clockwise from top right: an attic, lined with a hand-blocked Morris & Co. paper by Atelier d'Offard; a new bedroom in the east wing; and two views of a new panelled guest bedroom and bathroom, with antique bed hangings bought from Peta Smyth.

above and opposite The new swimming pool building in the east garden is designed to read as an eighteenth-century orangery, inspired a little by Robert Adam's building at Croome Court in Worcestershire. A tall Doric façade in Bath stone has double-hung sash windows, which pocket into the ceiling so that you can walk through into the garden beyond. We designed the interior in a restrained neoclassical palette of cool marble, stone and plaster. The garden was designed by Pip Morrison and is richly planted in shades of white, cream, apricot and blue.

Regency Fireworks

WILTSHIRE, 2013

English Decoration was my first book, and as I describe in the introduction it brought enquiries from interesting people intrigued by some of the things I was saying about old houses. One of the first calls was to see this dazzling little manor house in Wiltshire, a classical architectural dream.

I don't think I'd ever seen a house with such richly ornate plasterwork compressed into such a delicate, pocket-scaled building. Wonderful ceilings and sophisticated columns of great delicacy; a Gothick stable block; a thatched dairy filled with delft tiles; a cottage orné at the entrance to the driveway: it was a perfect, sleeping gem.

Construction works were due to start imminently, and I was being asked to decorate. I am afraid I committed the cardinal sin of stepping on toes immediately, because there was a beautiful, tiny, cobbled courtyard with various sheds and outbuildings around it. A plan had been formulated by the architect to glaze it over and remove the 'sheddery'. Now I am afraid there is nothing I love more than a cobbled yard, and old country house sheds. I sketched a little remodel on the way home on the train, and made it a condition of taking on the job that the glass roof didn't live to see the light of day. So it came to pass.

The owners loved the building, but they wanted to bring to it a sense of colour, scale and light that was somehow different from the classic idea of 'English country house taste'. They had lived for decades in Hong Kong, had a collection of dynamic contemporary art and were certainly not afraid of strong colour. Together, we worked our way through the rooms, simple here, rich there, bright here, soft for a moment. The combination worked. The builders were far behind schedule, and I think it was probably the most stressful pre-Christmas installation of our lives, but thanks to the remarkable efforts of my assistant Lucy Wilks, and our very junior assistant Luke Edward Hall (who you could tell already was destined for great things), we got there.

I visited after a few years to take photographs for this book. So much life had happened here already, but something gave me particular joy: the arrival of the ping-pong table and table football in the double-square, columned entrance hall. This is a room that we never quite knew what to do with: very beautiful, very unlived-in. Now it's the heart of the home, and that, for me, is what it's really all about.

opposite A delicately curved Ionic porch, in warm sandstone, invites you into the long hall beyond. A passage leads straight through the house to the east garden. The property underwent a huge restoration, but we managed to preserve the feeling of untouched age with these stone façades.

following pages The hall is a beautiful, long, low-ceilinged room with double fireplaces and Doric columns framing the front door. It began as a rather austere space, furnished with only the pair of wing chairs upholstered in electric blue silk (bought from Max Rollitt), a round hall table and the fireplace fender you see in the foreground. It was a lovely room, but curiously unused. After a few months, the family installed the ping-pong table (serendipity had it that the colour perfectly matches Max's chairs) and table football. Now it is never empty – just how I like this sort of room to be.

opposite and above The drawing room has an amazing 'tented' Regency plaster ceiling. Originally, just one half of the room (above left) had the plaster ceiling, and the other half was a delicate, glass-roofed conservatory. What a beautiful space that must have been! But at some stage in the early twentieth century, the conservatory was removed, the room doubled in size and a perfect replica of the plaster ceiling created. The room is sunny and filled with light and colour, although in very many ways the core ingredients of the interior are gentle and muted. The pops come from cushions and from the needlepoint ottoman that I designed, which was stitched for us by the charity Fine Cell Work.

opposite The plasterwork riches extend to the stair hall, with slender fluted Corinthian columns. I wanted to give this tall, narrow space a sense of scale and drama, and we painted it in strong, architectural 'Cooks Blue' from Farrow & Ball, with crisp white on the plaster and woodwork. The walls are lined with our clients' collection of striking contemporary art.

right The fine Regency mahogany handrail and oak staircase. I designed and coloured this runner, closely based on a David Hicks original.

following pages The laundry room, largely untouched, which we painted in Farrow & Ball 'Blue Ground'. We restored the original laundry pulley and installed a chequerboard floor of salvaged black and red Victorian quarry tiles. The kitchen, designed by Plain English, is painted in lipstick-toned 'Atomic Red' by Little Greene.

PURE MILK
PURE BUTTER

above The principal bathroom is papered in Zuber's 'Bamboo' – the room is a little homage to the eye-catching cover of the September 2012 issue of *The World of Interiors*, which featured a Parisian bathroom by Franz Potisek. This room is spacious and comfortable, with a deep free-standing bathtub. Behind me as I took this photograph is a tall run of wardrobes we designed. We thought carefully about forming a separate small dressing room, but on balance a generous scale felt better.

opposite The bedroom next door has calm and restful ingredients: a classic wallpaper by de Gournay, a four-poster bed by Beaudesert, woven-jute flooring and simple linen curtains. Decoration doesn't need to be complicated or overly clever to feel right.

Highland Drama

SCOTLAND, 2018

The area of the Highlands near the estate of Balmoral is perhaps the most achingly beautiful part of Scotland. Here, Rupert Cunningham, the studio's senior design director, added a new wing to an ancient tower house, for a younger generation taking on an ancestral home.

The castle has a tumultuous history, with huge building works in the eighteenth and nineteenth centuries swelling the edifice in scale. Fortunes turning, it suffered almost complete ruin in the twentieth century. But in the 1970s, in one of the great conservation triumphs of the century, the Victorian extensions were removed, and the tower house creatively restored, once again becoming home to the family that has owned it for the last 650 years. New walled gardens were planted and woodland re-established at the centre of the estate. Life breathed here again.

Forty years later, a new generation was taking on the mantle. The younger family members wanted to give the building something it never had: a generous, warm, family kitchen and sitting room, and conceived the idea of a long, low wing to the side of the old tower, providing some much-needed guest rooms above, as well as a new forecourt behind.

They worked initially with the distinguished architect Nicholas Groves-Raines, one of the leading figures of the traditional architectural movement in Scotland, but after concept planning was achieved, they had a pause before starting with Rupert to bring their vision to life. The scheme had moved forward in their minds, and Rupert's brief was to stitch together the disparate parts of the castle with a dramatic new top-lit stair hall that brings the whole house together with a powerful architectural voice. A double-height arcade allowed him to consolidate the many shapes and corners into a single piece.

The architectural language is of the gentle Scottish vernacular–classical tradition, with a steeply pitched roof of reclaimed Westmorland slate, and walls in rough harling with natural stone detailing. Rupert brought his remarkable light touch of intelligent, fine detailing to every corner of the building, often transmitted at a distance, with site visits few and far between, as the building work took place throughout eighteen months of the Covid pandemic. It became rather like building in the old way, when the renowned Edwardian architects were utterly dependent, for remote projects, on the skill and care of the builder and the clerk of works, both of whose qualities we had in abundance here. Today, it is hard to tell where the new and old come together, a house for the ages, settled in its place – safe, now, for generations to come.

opposite The new sandstone doorway designed by Rupert with seventeenth-century moulded detailing, leads into a new and welcoming panelled hall, painted in 'Sudbury Yellow' by Farrow & Ball.

following pages At dusk in the Scottish midsummer, the castle glows in the half-light. Rupert's new wing, containing the family room and kitchen with guest bedrooms above, forms a gentle and inevitable piece of this ancient composition. A wonderful setting of parkland trees and lawn leads to meadow in the foreground, with a wide stream as the boundary between the two.

above The crowstepped gable in the foreground is brand new, with the old towers of the castle – restored in the 1970s from a near ruin – beyond. The recent work, with local sandstone dressings and a roof of reclaimed Westmorland slate, settles completely into the whole. This elevation faces the new rear service courtyard.

opposite A view from the old castle to the new wing, showing Rupert's brilliant attention to detail. The dormers are carefully styled in an early classical manner and contain the initials of the various titles of the family who live here. Note the gutterless roofline in the traditional Scottish vernacular, designed to avoid either a forest of downpipes or a gutter running in front of all the raised wall dormers.

above and opposite At the centre of the castle, Rupert designed this astonishing double-height stair hall, which is nestled between the vast existing stair tower and the main bulk of the castle. The stairs needed not only to pick up the lower levels of the old castle, but also to serve the much higher level of the new west wing. The screen of arches was conceived to rationalise the central volume into a cube, with a tall, top-lit ceiling. The geometry and drama of this space are only hinted at by this photograph, and the whole unified by the rich emerald 'Egyptian Green', by Papers and Paints, chosen by Kate Arbuthnott, who helped our clients with the decoration. The chimneypiece is from Jamb.

Restoration Story

DORSET, 2015

This is Chettle, among the finest of the English Baroque houses, a restless, breathtaking, bold building by the hand of Thomas Archer, and one of the architectural gems of Dorset. For decades the house had slipped into increasingly great decay, until finally a new chapter began.

The house is at the centre of a large estate, on the edge of a sleepy, little-touched village in Dorset. But the vagaries of inheritance had detached the house and its small acreage from the estate around it. Divided into flats, the building had fallen into a spiral of disrepair. The roof was in terrible condition, the windows disintegrating and the upper floors had mostly been abandoned; in the basement, rising damp had led to a strange decision to build a new, raised floor several feet above the old. By any standards, this was a project that would require patience and energy, both of which the house fortunately found in its remarkable new owners, Tom and Rosamond Sweet-Escott.

Tom and Rosamond had begun to assemble a team that already included my friends landscape architect Pip Morrison and architect Hugh Petter, who would be leading the restoration of the building fabric. We were to design and detail the new interior works, and help with colours, furnishings and furniture. From the first meeting, Tom and Rosamond made it clear that they wanted a relaxed, happy, friendly house, with rooms that would respect its esteemed history, but without being too stuffy, or feeling like a museum. They talked about rooms with rich colour and pattern, and a sense of playfulness and fun: a brief we relished.

Our ideas evolved slowly, and we had plenty of time as the long and complex process of repairing and restoring the house took shape under Hugh's control. We spent happy days choosing colours and wallpapers. Tom and Rosamond had a lifetime's collection of furniture and paintings and enjoyed filling the gaps. The assembling of the interiors was not an instant thing, laid out on a plate; we brought in the first pieces and added layers where needed. This is a process that will, if I know Tom, doubtless continue forever – just as it should. I would be dismayed by the thought that the day I leave a house is the moment after which nothing changes or evolves.

Tom and Rosamond have become real friends. Charlie and I have spent many a summer's evening at Chettle, with the beautiful sight and sound of the swifts and swallows arcing and wheeling above the house, dipping into the reflecting pond made by Pip, the walls and roof once again repaired for the generations to come. I think how lucky they were to find this house, and it them.

opposite A combination of two of my favourite patterns: Morris & Co.'s 'Willow Bough' and 'Magnolia' by GP & J Baker – not the first time I used these together, and certainly not the last. Together they make this room warm and friendly, a crucial part of bringing the family kitchen into one of the grand spaces of the *piano nobile*. Beyond is a glimpse of the kitchen itself, with antique delft tiles above the range and warm orange walls painted in 'The Long Room' by Paint & Paper Library.

following pages The west front of Chettle glows in autumnal afternoon sunshine. Archer's extraordinary Baroque composition is at its finest here, with curved corners and fanciful stone capitals based on examples by the Italian architect Francesco Borromini in Rome, which we can assume Archer would have seen. Today, Chettle is settled and serene in its landscape, but how remarkable this house must have seemed when it emerged from the ground right at the beginning of the eighteenth century. Pip Morrison has revealed and restored a lost Baroque landscape stretching out all around the house and into the countryside beyond.

left Archer's soaring double-height stair hall, with the original oak sash windows, beautifully restored and put into full working order under the supervision of restoration architect Hugh Petter. We treated this space in a gentle way, in shades of white and stone. Thick olive-green velvet curtains help to create warmth on a winter's evening.

opposite above The stone hall, facing west, has curved corners and original early eighteenth-century plasterwork. We painted this room in shades of stone. The original floor was carefully lifted, underfloor heating installed below, and reset. The double doors, on axis with the main entrance in the stair hall, lead to a wide beech avenue stretching 550 yards into the park.

opposite below The oak staircase (left); a hall (right) is lined with a coral-coloured hand-blocked wallpaper by the American firm Adelphi Hangings, with whom we work on many of our projects. The double door leads into a small WC, which we introduced at this corner, and the tall door to the left opens into the drawing room seen on the following pages.

right This room was knocked together from a series of smaller spaces in the mid-nineteenth century, when the then-owners decreed that Chettle needed a ballroom. It had a forlorn quality, and our clients Rosamond and Tom Sweet-Escott had a strong desire to create a new panelled room that would have something of the original quality. We retained the nineteenth-century cornice and ceiling, but everything else is new. The decoration evokes the classic, comfortable, richly coloured world of the English country house drawing room, with my favourite colours of coral, olive, soft warm grey and dashes of burnt orange and lime green.

following pages In the dining room we packed a punch with Farrow & Ball's 'St Giles Blue', which Rosamond had seen in our dining room at home, and loved. The curtains are in 'Pertelote' by GP & J Baker, a fabric that I believe is now unfortunately out of print. The rocking horse is a family heirloom. The William IV sideboard was bought for £500 from Jack Laver Brister, one of the luminaries of the young antique-dealing world – as always, remarkably well priced.

left A guest bedroom is painted in the soft, inviting 'Pink Ground' from Farrow & Ball, designed to look lovely by lamplight for guests arriving after dark. The curtains are in 'Arcadia' by Christopher Moore, a fabric especially recoloured for us for this project. From here, the decoration evolved. Tom wanted an antique bed for the room, and eventually we found this beautiful example from dealer James Graham-Stewart. Its painted ivy canopy frame inspired the bathroom wallpaper and I was happy to locate a few yards of a discontinued ivy chintz fabric on eBay that we made into the bedspread. Sharp-eyed readers will spot that the bamboo cane settee is on loan from its normal place in the bay window at the Old Parsonage (pages 274–5). When the house was photographed for *The World of Interiors* in the summer of 2019, this was the only piece of furniture we hadn't yet found.

Neoclassical Purity

SOUTHERN ENGLAND, 2017

Here is a remarkable place, ancient in character. It was the site of a lost house, surrounded by a wide moat, at the heart of an enormous estate with veteran oaks and expansive parkland. It was a project not without challenges, the first of which being that the new owner had taken on an abandoned construction site.

It is hard to explain the sight that met me on my first visit here: a raw steel frame and vast concrete basement that – as an essential part of our brief – had to be retained. We were asked to enter a limited architectural competition for the project. This is not something I normally like to do, because I feel it is a very strange way to choose an architect: so much depends not on a single initial design, but on a sense of shared connection between land, vision and process. I always say to people, you really don't need to *like* your architect, but you do both need to trust one another implicitly, and that's something intuitive rather than something gleaned from looking at a drawing on a sheet of paper.

But in this instance the challenge was more than I could resist. The parameters were completely set: the dimensions of the building were fixed, without room for negotiation, by that insane steel frame and by the form of the previous planning approval. I love a task with such defined limits, taking an ugly duckling and trying to turn it into a swan. I set about drawing four potential versions: Jacobean (with tall, leaded-light windows), Baroque, Palladian, and an ideal of cool neoclassicism. Such fun – like playing scales on the piano for practice.

It was quite strange to find that we had been chosen, with our final design, and thus we embarked on a project to create a new neoclassical palace of refined detail. Rupert Cunningham and I began in earnest, assisted by many of the skilled architects and draughtspeople in the office. We adopted an architectural language not often used by classical architects today: a pure neoclassical style, deeply infused with the late eighteenth-century work of the Adam brothers. We visited and measured houses and interiors, studied their books and learnt much in the process. There is a huge, top-lit, stone stair hall and plaster halls, and great rooms of display, with a physical scale that one doesn't often get to work with today.

The quality of the building work is absolutely the equal of its eighteenth-century counterparts. Now, all this building needs is the ingredient of time: two hundred years of moss and lichen, weather and softening. These photographs, taken just before our client moved in, represent a fleeting moment – austere, cool and pure – like a still pond before a pebble is thrown in. The rest will follow.

opposite The stone staircase was created in a traditional manner, with each riser built into a solid brick surrounding wall as the construction work proceeded. The shape of the scroll ends forms a beautiful rhythm when seen from below. Together with the ironwork, painted in a dark gunmetal blue, the mouldings and details were based on an eighteenth-century staircase by Robert Adam at Osterley Park.

following pages The new house on a misty autumnal morning. The moat and corner 'pepper-pot' pavilion are original, as is the crenellated wing to the rear. The new building draws close inspiration from several houses by Robert Adam, with attenuated Ionic columns to the south elevation and restrained stonework detailing to the east front, facing a newly replanted parterre garden.

previous pages The new entrance hall. We detailed every element of the interior of the house at full scale. Here, scallop-fluted Doric columns and entablature are formed in plasterwork made by expert plasterers Locker & Riley, who completed all the plaster in the house. Paired doors pocket into reveals, and a stone floor was installed with tight butt joints – very hard to achieve with modern construction tolerances.

opposite Clockwise from top left: a detail of the new stone fireplace in the entrance hall, designed by Rupert and made for us by Jamb; the upper stair landing; the staircase showing the scroll-end stone treads and the elegant pattern they form from below.

right The central stair hall is top lit with a huge oculus, flooding the middle of the house with natural daylight. A series of openings and bedroom corridors leads from the central gallery, with views across it and to the ground floor below – a dynamic and interesting space, which changes dramatically as you move around the house.

following pages The south front, from the park, with fine veteran oaks. To the left is the restored Regency ironwork bridge over the moat.

Ancestral Voices

SCOTLAND, 2010–

This is an ancient house. Like many of our projects, it started in a rather unplanned way. The owners, who knew other clients of ours, were rewiring and were wondering if the rooms should be repainted in the same colours as before. Would I come and have a look?

There was something mildly magnificent about the uniform 1930s soft pea-green paintwork on everything: walls, skirtings, architraves, dado, panelling, everywhere other than the cornice, which was pure white. But I knew that subtle new colours would bring this beautiful neoclassical house to life. I made some suggestions and we tried out samples, and thus began a project that has lasted more than a decade and will probably never quite finish.

In the rooms that we have finished, we've been quite radical. The biggest reordering began with the creation of a new drawing room, in what had been the dining room since the early nineteenth century. That was a bold change, but one which has worked perfectly. It was such a curious decision on the part of the nineteenth-century architect to put the dining room in the largest room, with windows facing north, east and south, and to have the drawing room on the side of the house facing north. Once the change was made, it felt inevitable.

The drawing room feels as if it has been here forever, but it was first put together the week before this photograph was taken. The space had been a building site for months beforehand as plasterwork was stripped and cleaned and old windows and shutters were repaired. Authenticity in atmosphere is a question not only of age, but also of value. And, on closer inspection, we see that there is a strange tangerine flash to the curtain lining. Well, I've recently embraced the colour tangerine – combined with lemon yellow, and a palette of cool grey and warm fruitwood tones, as you see here, it simply cannot be beaten. The sofa is a lovely burnt caramel, to complete the mix.

The sun streams in and a contented dog finds a warm spot. Somehow this is what makes this room come awake. It's alive, of course, with the voices of many ancestors, and the taste of ages, reverberating through time, but this house of history is alive in a different way too now, with a degree of happy freshness, greeting the world each morning.

opposite This room had originally been the dining room. Facing north, east and south, it was one of the brightest rooms which felt completely wasted on a room normally used in the evenings and only then on grand occasions. After much discussion we decided to swap the use of this room with that of the north-facing drawing room, the latter becoming the new dining room (see page 220). To emphasise a feeling of lightness and warmth, we upholstered the walls in a delicate oyster-white linen and used a sunny-yellow silk for the curtains. The room feels as if it has been here forever, but in fact it was finished about a week before this photograph was taken – the pictures are not all yet hung.

following pages We repainted the hall in three shades of stone grey. Existing sofas were given new blue velvet cushions, and a new ottoman and silk lampshades draw on the bright red coat of the overmantel portrait. This is a north-facing room, but I woke up at dawn in the middle of summer to take this shot – we are in Scotland, so the sun was streaming in for a few minutes. On wintry afternoons, by a roaring fire, it is a lovely place for tea.

The Jewelry of Southeast

opposite Formerly the drawing room, now the dining room. I chose 'Teresa's Green' from Farrow & Ball for the walls, a gentle colour that looks beautiful by day or night, and which works perfectly with the old brown velvet curtains that we rehung from the former dining room next door. The frieze was picked out in an Etruscan pink, and we selected brown silk shades for the lamps. The existing dining room rug fitted the new room perfectly.

above Relaxed clutter in the sitting room at day's end. We selected comfortable George Sherlock sofas and a blue silk lampshade. The candlestick is a present from Pentreath & Hall.

opposite Clockwise from top left: the gents' loo, with original hand-blocked Morris & Co. 'Willow Bough' wallpaper; the Chinese bedroom, newly papered in a beautiful chinoiserie paper from Allyson McDermott, with a 1970s fitted carpet and an old pair of curtains from another bedroom in the house; a redecorated guest bedroom with a custom coloured print of Jean Monro's legendary 'Hydrangea and Rose' chintz, and the walls painted in '5-063' from Papers and Paints; the guest bathroom next door, painted in 'Parsonage Pink' from Papers and Paints, with its original bathtub and a collection of prints found in an attic.

right This stair hall was repainted in an archive Farrow & Ball colour, 'Dix Blue' – a fine backdrop to a great collection of family portraits.

A Jacobean Castle Revived

CORNWALL, 2018–

This story begins with a tragic fire that ripped through this magical house in the late 1980s. All that remained were the ancient Jacobean walls; the floors, ceilings and roof were entirely burnt through. The house needed to be completely rebuilt.

The building stands in a remarkable position on the Lynher River, opposite another great Cornish house, Antony. It is a dreamlike place surrounded by beautiful gardens created over decades by the previous owners. That couple had carried out a huge post-fire restoration, supervised by Anthony Jaggard, one of an early band of neoclassical architects practising in the 1980s. Thirty years on, it was time for them to sell. The estate was bought by our clients, an ebullient young family originally from South Africa.

Our first conversations were prompted by thinking about a significant remodelling. We considered major alterations to a service wing and looked at reconfiguring parts of the interior to bring a more Jacobean, or indeed Arts and Crafts, flavour to the building, which was still Grade I listed despite the damage wrought by the fire. We started successful discussions with Historic England, and began to move towards an application.

I well recall my last site visit to the castle in March 2020, just a few days before the first Covid pandemic lockdown. Our clients had arrived the night before. With prescience, they were leaving London and moving to Cornwall. The following week, the world changed. As with so many other projects, things shifted into a strange gear.

We stayed closely in touch. As the family settled in, and the magic of the place worked upon them, priorities gently adapted to new circumstance. They realised they were happy with many of the things we'd previously talked about altering. We began to ask whether we could work without employing the wrecking ball or instigating years of planning applications and months of demolition followed by months of rebuilding. The architectural project became less creative, but the rich potential of good old-fashioned decorating stepped in. And so it was that we left everything alone, and got out the paint brush and wallpaper paste, and started finding furniture and furnishings. There's an object lesson for us all here.

How many wars and plagues have these ancient walls seen? There is something so reassuring about knowing that however bad circumstances seem, everything has always happened before and will always come good in the end. I was the last person to visit the castle before the pandemic struck, and curiously I was the first person back when it was over. Time passes, and things heal – the lesson of all magnificent old houses.

opposite A late eighteenth-century cabinet in the guest bedroom corridor reflects the early Georgian portrait shown on page 233 (bottom left). I am fascinated by the thin wobbly glass in fine old furniture: imagine finding such a beautiful quality of work today!

following pages We have seen the combination of Morris & Co.'s 'Willow Bough' and GP & J Baker's 'Magnolia' before – in the kitchen at Chettle, shown on page 195. Here, the atmosphere is completely different, but just as pleasing. A custom-made round table fits next to the curved window seat, and we found warm Rainer Daumiller 1970s chairs to complete the group. The floor is in a linoleum check. The red schoolhouse lamps had been in my old office. The kitchen joinery was introduced during the 1980s renovation, and we decided to keep it, with a repaint and a refresh of hardware. I am a strong believer in leaving things alone if possible, and this house is a fine example of that philosophy.

God's
Oliver
Cromwell
and the
Weidenfeld
& Nicolson
THE

left The dining room is on the low-ceilinged ground floor. The cornice and joinery were part of the 1980s reconstruction by Jaggard and have a nice early flavour to them. We painted the walls in a rich orange, 'The Long Room' by Paint & Paper Library, and bought a fine collection of nineteenth-century furniture: a handsome Aesthetic Movement sideboard and dining chairs designed by Augustus Pugin. The owners' collection of blue-and-white china is striking against this wall.

following pages In the drawing room, on the high-ceilinged *piano nobile*, we hung the walls in an oyster-coloured linen. The neoclassical sofa shown in the foreground came from Hawker Antiques, covered in bottle-green silk, and a pair of 'Grosvenor' sofas from Howard & Sons are on either side of the original marble chimneypiece. This is a generously scaled room. The eighteenth-century portrait was bought from the Jasper Conran sale at Christie's, and the abstract painting on the right-hand wall is by Michel Mouffe. The mirrors are original to the house. I couldn't resist adding a splash of purple to the mix in the new silk lampshades.

Meier

AXEL VERVOORDT
A World of Design
HELMUT NEWTON

left A calm and restful palette in the principal bedroom: dragged paper 'DR 1261' from Farrow & Ball, 'Fez Weave' from Guy Goodfellow on the armchair and 'Aurora' curtain fabric from Paolo Moschino. A Chinese export lacquer cabinet holds a garniture of serene delft vases. A shot of colour is provided by the cerulean-blue silk lampshade.

opposite Clockwise from top left: a view from the blue guest room across a lime-green corridor into a child's bedroom papered in David Hicks's 'Vase' wallpaper; the corridor densely hung with prints by GiovannI Battista Piranesi; bright yellow silk lampshades and a chintz, 'Hydrangea and Rose', from Jean Monro, in the blue guest room, painted in 'Lulworth Blue' from Farrow & Ball; a detail of an eighteenth-century portrait and frame, bought at the Jasper Conran sale at Christie's. The colour of the gentleman's coat inspired the tablecloth in the corridor.

right Astonishingly, in the Chinese bedroom, the original eighteenth-century hand-painted wallpaper survived the catastrophic fire that started here. The paper was severely damaged but underwent a careful restoration by skilled expert Allyson McDermott. The top section was destroyed completely, so it was rehung two feet higher, with the introduction of a new dado rail. There was no question that we would keep the paper. To the right of the door, some unsympathetic modern joinery was removed and replaced with the new arched opening into a dressing closet, and we had some lengths of matching paper painted by Mathew Bray and Matthew Collins. The room has a gentle character, with shots of colour provided by the bold silk lampshades and Chinese-inspired fabrics from Clarence House on the footstool and Le Manach on the bed cushions.

following pages Soft, autumnal light in the garden – roses and dahlias still flourishing in the balmy Cornish climate. The ancient house is crenellated, with four corner turrets providing tiny guest bedrooms on each level. The bedroom on the previous pages leads on to this garden through the right-hand French doors. It is hard to imagine that, thirty years ago, this house, layered by time, was completely burnt out by a terrible fire.

Tangerine Dream

JERSEY, CHANNEL ISLANDS, 2018

I was approached to decorate a new house being planned for a spectacular site on the island of Jersey. It was a striking design, but as I thought about the interior flow, I realised that I wanted to make some significant changes. I dared to ask the question, because as far as I'm concerned, nothing is fixed until the building work starts.

At that point, if you are sensible, you stop making changes. Change on-site is the enemy of progress. But until then, while you are thinking on paper, I do believe anything is worth saying.

The design was for a handsome Regency stucco villa, with the concept plans developed by my friend, the architect Hugh Petter, but as I played around with the potential for the interior, I realised we could have some serious architectural fun not necessarily anticipated by the planning drawings. The idea of a top-lit staircase bubbled on my drawing board and wouldn't go away. I sent some scribbles to my client, who is someone happy taking a risk. He thought for a little and we were given the go-ahead. As we moved forward with design drawings, Rupert Cunningham in our studio made more changes, and so I think it's true to say the authorship of this building is one of many hands. It's so often the way in building, and increasingly I steer clear of the idea of the architect as a lone, staggering genius. But it is good to have fun, and we really have here – hopefully, based on especially solid foundations.

We built the house during one of the Covid pandemic lockdowns – like a few of the others in these pages – and Jersey was a completely closed place. Many were the video calls that resolved small details and problems. When it came to decorate, I was painting colours on the walls of my imagination. Videos and photographs go only so far. The client has bold taste, and together he and I enjoyed going a little crazy. The central staircase could have looked beautiful in a muted palette, but that wouldn't have been him at all. I suggested, inspired by the vivid palettes of Irish houses such as Glin Castle or the work of David Hicks at Baronscourt, a saturated tangerine against pure white plasterwork. Astonishingly, he agreed. The same colour lands as a squashy orange sofa in the sitting room, resplendent on a coral and sky-blue tartan carpet. Genuinely, this is complex, serious architecture combined with irreverent, vibrant decoration. The results are electric, a house that fizzes with strength and joy, just how I think it should be.

opposite Rupert detailed this fine Greek Doric door surround for the house in an austerely restrained manner, with scallop-fluted column shafts. Much of the woodwork, including this element, was made by Scope Joinery of Norfolk, and brought out to Jersey for installation. The front door leads through to the tangerine-orange top-lit stair hall shown on the following pages, and beyond that to the breakfast room. Glazed doors open to the east front with astonishing views to the sea, and to France on the horizon.

above and opposite The top-lit stone stair hall, which forms the dramatic, architectural heart of the house, has vistas in all directions. The columns are made of plaster by Stevensons of Norwich to our design, employing the 'Tower of the Winds' order – appropriate for this house, on the shore of the island of Jersey, which can be an extremely windy site (on the days we were taking photographs, we were in the middle of a force 10 gale for much of the time). The stairs are in Portland stone with metal balusters and a slender mahogany handrail. We decided on the bright orange walls ('Spindle Tree' from the Werner's Nomenclature range by Papers and Paints) to inject a shock of Pop-toned colour into what could have been an austerely classical space. Our client has a great sense of fun, and the decoration is designed to reflect that.

opposite Clockwise from top left: a Wedgwood urn on one of a pair of consoles in the dining room, with doors leading to the library shown on this page; the drawing room, with armchairs in Veere Grenney's 'Folly' fabric and a yellow ottoman to our design; the snug, leading from the kitchen, with a jolly tartan carpet, one sofa in tangerine linen, the other in 'Paw Print' from Soane Britain. The walls are in 'Blue Ground' from Farrow & Ball, and the curtains are in 'Vegetable Tree' designed by Josef Frank for Svenskt Tenn.

right The library with its beautiful Regency detailing and delicate 'Erddig Small Stair' cornice that I designed many years ago for Stevensons of Norwich. The curtains are in a classic Michael S. Smith stripe, 'Indian Flower'. The walls are finished in a burnt-caramel velvet.

following pages A view from the kitchen, with its restrained Regency detailing by our studio, and pantry and glassware cabinets built into the wall on either side of a shallow segmental arch leading to the breakfast room. A square-headed niche makes a home for our client's painted dresser. The ceiling light is from Svenskt Tenn and the chairs – another staple of many of our projects – are the original 'Wishbone' design by Hans J. Wegner. Light floods in from the doors that you see on page 239.

PARIS A L'AGE CLASSIQUE

above and opposite The villa has five bays, with two single-storey wings. The walls are in a natural lime render, which will gently age. If the effect of the weather is too severe in this exposed Jersey location, the walls can be limewashed with a shelter coat. During the construction, the client decided to add a balcony to this elevation to enjoy the views over to the French coast. We detailed the architecture with attenuated Greek Doric columns and delicate Regency metalwork. Rain and storms were sweeping through when we visited the house to take these photographs, and here it is, washed and sparkling, in a moment of bright sunshine.

An Exuberant Palette

HAMPSHIRE, 2018

In a watery bit of Hampshire, on the edge of a beautiful village surrounded by meandering chalk streams and flood meadows, is an old manor house. Filled with laughter, it is home to a vivacious family of energetic parents and four young boys who hurtle around the house and garden.

I was brought here by my friends Bridget Elworthy and Henrietta Courtauld, the genius duo behind The Land Gardeners, who do everything from designing and growing blowsy flower gardens to creating climate-friendly compost, all in a whirlwind of endless energy. Bridget and Henrietta had been asked by the owners, Charlotte Dellal and her husband Maxim, to help them conceive visions for garden and meadows. They then realised that they needed help with the house and interiors too, and so began an adventure where our ideas bounced around creative minds like popcorn jumping out of the pan.

Charlotte's eye is impeccable, and she knew exactly what she liked and didn't, but I think it's true to say that it was in the combination of ideas that we excelled at working together. She wanted a home filled with bright colour and contrasts, but it's a building that finds moments of great restraint, too. This is a generous, overflowing house for parties, with a huge dining room, buttercup-yellow drawing room and a west-facing library that we glazed in a moss-green lacquer, but it has its quiet spaces as well, in which to sit, write, think or linger.

The restoration was an epic undertaking, carried out with the help of a diligent local architect, but under our watchful eye. We worked our way through rooms and furnishings, all the while making sure this was a house that could be grown into: Charlotte was adamant, quite rightly, that she didn't want to live somewhere delivered on a plate where everything was finished in one instant. We left gaps on walls and spaces in rooms, where pictures and furniture would one day find a place. I took these photographs a few years after move-in, and things have already evolved since then. That is how I like it, and just how you'll find it if you work on decorating a house with me.

When it's all put together in this way, the one thing that exudes from the happy beating heart of a house is the personality of those who live there. It's this creative energy, between all these ideas, from room to room, and from house to garden and back again, that makes my life as a decorator so interesting. Wearing my architectural hat, I restore the bones, revealing the structure and healing the building. Decoration is about the messy, bright, cheerful thing called life, which covers all that up again, and makes it real, vital and unique.

opposite A favourite Mauny wallpaper in the downstairs cloakroom. With its fireplace and woodburning stove, this is a welcoming little room. You glimpse through to the stair hall beyond, to the archway shown on the following page.

left The stair hall is painted in Farrow & Ball's 'Pink Ground', a beautiful warm plaster-like colour. The view beyond is to the glamorous library, shown on the opposite page. Glazed and lacquered olive-green walls – painted for us by Mathew Bray and Matthew Collins – glow in an astonishing way in the afternoon sunlight. The wicker urn is from Atelier Vime, and the curtains are in an exotic silk stripe from Robert Kime.

opposite The fireplace was existing, in a stripped neoclassical pine – of course, originally it would have been painted, but we enjoyed its warmth and feeling of age. We added a new club fender with a bright turquoise horsehair seat. Armchairs are upholstered in Michael S. Smith's 'Grace' chintz, and a BenI Ourain rug sits on the seagrass floor. We designed the large library bookcase, which also houses a television.

BEATON
ROME, MILAN, AND FABIO MAURI
ANDY WARHOL: THE COMPLETE COMMISSIONED MAGAZINE
DECADES A Century of Fashion
CAMERON SILVER

left The drawing room is in an egg-yolk yellow: sunny by day, warm and inviting by night. This is a comfortable room, with deep squashy Howard & Sons sofas, designed for conversation and relaxation. The one in the foreground is in a Charles Burger chintz, 'Fleurs de Pommiers'. We introduced new French doors leading out to the west garden. Charlotte and Maxim have a ravishing collection of pictures.

following pages In the dining room, we started with a glamorous, mirror-topped table in painted gesso designed and made for us by Jerry Rothman. Dinners in this room sparkle with candlelight. We sourced a large set of 'Cockpen' dining chairs, upholstered in the palest pink linen, and painted the walls – like the dining room at Chettle, incidentally – in rich 'St Giles Blue' from Farrow & Ball. The curtain fabric is 'Lola Montez' by Madeleine Castaing, who also designed the rug. A charismatic family portrait watches over glittering occasions today.

left In the bar, we painted the ceiling in a glossy cherry red, and wallpapered the little room in a Fornasetti paper. Charlotte and Maxim's hospitality is renowned, and the bar cart is appropriately well stocked.

opposite The kitchen, with joinery by the studio, is painted in a cheery lime green from Dulux, combined with pale yellow 'Willow' paper from Morris & Co. The range is from Lacanche. This is a practical and hardworking kitchen.

following pages The principal bedroom has an elegant Madeleine Castaing stripe on the curtains, 'Rayure Fleurie', seen in many of our projects and in our own flat in London. The eiderdown is from Flora Soames, and the eighteenth-century sofa is upholstered in a delicate shell-blue silk. The seagrass matting is made luxurious by a soft and fluffy rug.

ray ike rio guy
CLEAN GUT
HEALING FOODS
1001 HOME REMEDIES
I KNOW HOW TO COOK
PLENTY
GINGER PIG MEAT BOOK

above A bold and boisterous military-themed paper by Kravet in the boys' bedroom, with a painted chest of drawers and a wonderful collection of bits and pieces, neatly arranged. The sofa glimpsed beyond, in the hallway, is in 'Palm Drop' by Beata Heuman.

opposite For this bedroom, we scanned a collection of eighteenth-century botanical engravings and wallpapered the room with the resulting prints. Tintin, Snowy and a collection of tiny lead Highland soldiers are more than at home on the original Regency chimneypiece.

CHAPTER FIVE

VILLAGE & FARM

VILLAGE & FARM

When I was young, we lived in a tiny village in West Dorset. In the 1970s it was an idyllic place: for my parents, certainly, the happiest place they ever lived in the many moves they made for my father's naval career. Everyone knew each other, doors were always unlocked, traffic on the village lane felt non-existent, and the gang of children of various ages who lived on our street would be roving around all summer long, pretty much without a care in the world. I used to cycle off with a friend, without our parents having an idea of where we were, sometimes to an old farm at the bottom end of the village, where we'd sit and make mud pies by the stream for hours on end. Strangely, I can still remember quite clearly the saddle stones of the old grain store in that wonderful farmyard filled with adventures.

previous pages One side of the new range of brick-and-flint buildings at the farmyard complex shown on pages 314–21: a gentle, and hopefully seamless, addition to a fine group of nineteenth-century agricultural buildings.

Twenty-five years later I found myself returning almost to the place I'd grown up, in West Dorset, to the former parsonage in a hamlet called Littlebredy, at the eastern end of the Bride Valley, so called because the River Bride runs its length towards the sea, but vanishes underground before it reaches the coast. Village life here has been equally idyllic: not the hazy-tinted idyll of childhood memory, but of actual life, the here and now. Littlebredy is an estate village, with an ancient country house, Bridehead, at its heart, along with some forty cottages, an old walled garden, a village hall, and a village green and famous cricket ground made memorable in series of paintings by artist David Inshaw in the 1970s. All the houses are tenanted, and it has been my immense fortune to have found this house and for it to have found me in 2008, with Charlie coming to live here with me a few years later. It sounds like a place lost in time, but in fact it isn't; it's filled with young families and interesting people, but most of all, it's extraordinary fun. Many were the nights in the village hall when we danced on the bar in the small hours of the morning.

But even the best things change, and our years in Littlebredy may be coming to an end. Perhaps by the time *An English Vision* is published, we will be planning a move to our new house in Scotland, which is the final project in this book, as well as being by far the smallest house the studio has worked on. There, we will be even more remote, on the far west coast of Argyll, and with, I hope, many more adventures to come.

There's something about English village life that is extraordinarily special, but fragile too. In *The Village News: The Truth behind England's Rural Idyll* (2017), Tom Fort writes about the changing social forces that are moulding the village today, a narrative that's unsurprising to anyone living in the countryside. Farming – integral to the fabric of the real English village – is high on our political agenda as concerns about climate change, food production, national security, animal welfare and the environment play against a darkening background of pandemic and European war. Thatched roofs and leaded windows mask deeper concerns.

As architects, we circle the perimeter of so many decisions that make questions of design seem almost irrelevant: questions of justice, of environmental impact, materials, transport, longevity and the emotional value of place.

I've always tried to get through life by concentrating on the things that are in my power to control, and not to get depressed by the things that are not. Faced with the social and economic challenges of our world, it is easy to give up or give in. For me, this exercise becomes most thought-provoking in the small ecosystems of rural life, because these are places where individuals, or local groups, are really able to make a difference. Can we grow a village with meaning? What is the local economy, and what can our project do to support it? How do we provide new housing for young people in the countryside? And sometimes, it is still a question of aesthetics: what is the most inherent, most beautiful or appropriate building in this completely unspoilt landscape, because those are the buildings that will be loved and last longest, and those are the most sustainable over time.

I've written in previous pages that I have increasingly come to realise that buildings aren't the most important thing: the setting within the land, our relationship to topography, water, food production and materials have a far more powerful impact on what is going to feel right and wrong. Village and farm settlements grew slowly and organically over long periods, sometimes hundreds or even thousands of years. There is a quality to these settlements, and to their relationship with the agricultural hinterland, which has evolved as a living, changing organism, and will continue to do so.

Places, like organisms, are either growing or dying – change is dynamic; it is impossible, and dangerous, to try to keep things 'as they are'. But change can be good or bad in fragile systems. It is our job to distinguish, with both research-based *and* emotional knowledge, how we should best nurture this ancient–modern symbiosis for the future.

Villages and farms get us to the crux of how we live, and why – of mankind's place in the longest evolutionary cycle. They predate cities and towns, and I imagine will outlive them all. For better or for worse, they are the simplest places where humans, animals, landscape, food and ecosystems meet: the crucible of the distant future. I love building towns, and the social and economic exchange they generate. I love cities, the entire basis of great civilisations and culture of humanity. But the farm and the village were at the beginning of the human journey, and will most likely be at its end. So, it's a good place for our journey to culminate too, in our tiny bothy on the far west coast of Scotland, with our animals and our small patch of land that Charlie is starting to farm – where we imagine ourselves in the howling wind of a November evening, rain sweeping in, hunkering down, sheltered by the hill above us and by the Isle of Jura beyond, and farther on, the Atlantic, and the whole of time past, and the whole of time to come.

Familiar Territory

DORSET, 2008–

This is a house that has defined me as much as I have defined it: the Old Parsonage, a place that Charlie and I love so much, and which for many is familiar territory through my blog, or Instagram, and my previous books. It's a truly happy home. We've been here a long time.

I will never forget when I cast eyes again on the parsonage, at Easter in 2008. I was seeing it for the first time in twenty-five years. My best friend Ben from school had lived here in the 1970s and '80s, and it was a house I knew incredibly well as a child. Admittedly, there were rooms we never went into, but it was a strange and wonderful thing to be walking through spaces that I had last seen so long ago and which still remained so familiar.

The house had been abandoned for almost a year and had a cold feeling; the garden was overgrown, like in a storybook. I knew that it was calling me. I had met my landlord that morning, and he kindly left me with the keys for the weekend. I went back a few times, and on each occasion I realised all the more what a special place it was. I remember sitting on the churchyard wall, on Sunday evening, looking back at the house, thinking with such clarity how it was going to change my life – and it did.

Sixteen years later, it's a house with so many layers of meaning for me and for Charlie. As I have described in the introduction to this chapter, our time here may now be drawing to a close. We will miss the house immensely, but new people will come and it will live a new chapter in its long life.

The parsonage was built in the 1820s, in a ravishing location next to the church, itself a beautiful building at the heart of the picturesque estate village created over generations by the ancient Dorset family who own the estate. The house's design is plain: three down, three up. It's position, perched on the edge of a south-facing slope at the head of the Bride Valley, is what makes the house remarkable – views in and out, up and down the garden.

We like to spend most of the summer outdoors, Charlie in his exquisite garden, which is a creation like nothing else. The house plays second fiddle to the great symphony outside: gentle, quiet, always evolving and an inextricable part of our lives.

opposite The Old Parsonage is built into the side of a hill, and on the north side of the house a wonderfully worn flight of blue Lias stone steps leads up to the carriage drive. Leafy and overgrown, there is an old Regency iron gate, and beyond, our little Morris Minor 1000, which is our summer car for bumbling around the Dorset lanes.

following pages The entrance hall with a Gothic oak hall chair, one of a pair; the front door (shown on page 267) is to the left. The wallpaper is 'Malahide' by David Skinner, famously used by my hero David Mlinaric at Luggala in Ireland. Beyond is the kitchen, painted in a gloss egg-yolk yellow from Dulux. On an old sofa inherited from my parents, Enid snoozes. The fabric is a discontinued pattern from Sanderson. Charlie's china cupboard groans with junk-shop finds. The kitchen chair is upholstered in joyous 'Aralia' by Josef Frank for Svenskt Tenn.

CULTURAL SOCIETY
URTH PRIZE

Sel

ELIZABETH II
OF MEAT
and a Large Assortment of Plated Articles
About 800 Volumes of Books,
A LARGE TELESCOPE ON STAND
THE FURNITURE OF
18 BED & DRESSING ROOMS
EIGHT MAHOGANY WARDROBES
DECORATED PINE SUITES,
LAST NIGHT BUT THREE!
BENEFIT OF MR. KITE.
Three Classicists
SATURDAY
11TH JULY 2015, at
The Brideshead
Cricket Ground,
LITTLEBREDY
BEN & CHARLIE
WEDDING
SUPPER
JESS UPTON
ENTERTAINMENTS,
&LIVE CAMELS

TOWNSHIP OF
BURNHILL
RUSTIC FETE
A DONKEY RACE,
GRINNING MATCH.
BISCUIT BOLTING.
DIPPING FOR EELS.
CLIMBING A GREASY POLE,

Fig. III.
portico in forma piu grande. La tinta piu nera indica
l'esistente avanti l'incendio, e la piu leggiera ciocchè ri-
mase consumato dal medesimo. Fig. IV. G. Elevazione dell'
avanzo del portico, corrispondente alla pianta della fig. III.
H. Le due colonne di tinta piu leggiera già consumate dal
fuoco; ed alle quali Severo, e Caracalla supplirono coll'
si osserva nella fig. II. I. Colonne spettanti
di Giunone. L. Piano moderno di Ro-
M. Piano del portico a cui salivasi per gradi.
di una delle colonne del circondario del
secondo la sua posizione in una cantina del
fabbriche. O. Colonne internate ne' fon-
delle stesse fabbriche. P. Fondamento.
del portico.

previous pages The kitchen is where we spend much of our time. The old AGA was already in the house when I moved in. The dresser and kitchen table I bought on eBay. The floor is painted 'Hardwick White' from Farrow & Ball. I laid the floorboards over the existing concrete floor when I first arrived. Now they are beautifully worn, and feel as though they could have been there for centuries.

opposite and above The dining room is papered in the olive and turquoise colourway of 'Willow Bough', which I designed as part of my first collection for Morris & Co. The curtains are in 'Brer Rabbit' from the same Queen Square collection. The drawing above the fireplace is by our friend Oisin Byrne, and adds to the vibrant colour in the room.

following pages The drawing room is painted in a colour made famous by this room, 'Parsonage Pink' from Papers and Paints, specially mixed for me by Patrick Baty. The curtains are in brown ticking from Ian Mankin and the floor is covered in seagrass. The blue armchair is an original from Howard & Sons, bought for a song at a junk auction; the linen was dyed by Polly Lyster of Dyeworks. The room is cluttered, supremely relaxed and filled with sunshine.

David Hockney
ON FLOWERS AMY MERRICK
WILDFLOWERS FOR THE QUEEN
E ENGLISH GARDEN

DORSET
BY
ARTHUR
MEE
CHRYSANTHEMUMS.—MOLYNEUX
THE
ITALIAN
OF THE

previous pages Left: the main guest bedroom is painted in dark olive green '4-050' from Papers and Paints, described by my old boss Charles Morris as the colour of a freshly laid cowpat. I love it and use it in many projects. Right clockwise from top left: a corridor with a collection of Peter Hone plasters leads to Charlie's flower room; the bathroom, papered in my colourway of Morris & Co.'s 'Bird & Anemone'; an antique creamware candlestick in Charlie's and my bedroom; the stair landing in my sky-blue 'Willow Bough' wallpaper.

right In our small guest bedroom, Morris & Co.'s 'Marigold' wallpaper, in my chocolate and cream colourway from the Queen Square collection, makes a beautiful backdrop to Charlie's antique fern and leaf prints, bought at Portobello Road Market. On the chair is one of my blankets for Johnstons of Elgin, and in the chimneypiece, a collection of Peter Hone plaster fragments.

THE JOY OF ART
LASCAUX
CONTEMPORARY TRENDS

above We can't stop buying junk-shop china, and the habit is extremely out of control. At bottom left is a rather beautiful set of Flight & Barr nineteenth-century china, inherited from my grandmother.

opposite The clutter continues in Charlie's flower room, filled here with buckets of tulips waiting to be delivered to London. The plaster columns were a present from Stevensons of Norwich. Being hollow, they are surprisingly light and are a very simple way to add grandeur wherever needed.

following pages The west front of the parsonage at sunset in high summer, with Charlie's extraordinary cottage garden overflowing with blowsy, scented flowers.

The Romance of the Sea

WEST CORNWALL, 2019

In the far west of Cornwall, the farthest western tip of England, lies this ancient-feeling house in a hidden valley overlooking the sparkling sea – a place for which I have an immense affinity, so close to the home of my maritime Cornish ancestors.

'Old Cornwall' read the email's subject line, which I received one summer from my client, who was hoping to become the new owner. I think I won the commission because of my Cornish surname; after all, my ancestress Dolly was the last person to speak the native Cornish language as her mother tongue. My family grew up in Mousehole and Paul, just a few miles from this magical place.

The house is unusual, an Arts and Crafts creation that began life in the early twentieth century as little more than a seaside bungalow and which had grown incrementally over many building phases. Some of these were of real quality; others less so. The whole house had suffered for years from benign neglect, with a roof that was in decay, windows that were rotting and wiring that needed replacing.

We considered lots of approaches to the design, and arrived at a decision to change nothing on the exterior but to carry out a significant internal remodelling: opening up a series of formal but rather unlovely dining and sitting rooms, and bringing the kitchen away from a cold, north-facing corner designed solely for servants to cook meals to bring to rich people enjoying the sunshine and view. We kept and restored the best of the house, and at its core we created a spacious new family room, with kitchen at one end, dining table in the middle, and fireplace and seating at the other.

We felt that the spirit of this room didn't want to imitate the Arts and Crafts style of the old granite wings; instead, we created a lofty new ceiling, with pine beams and glossy white-painted boards, and a wall of French doors with clear views to the sea. The kitchen was designed with a distinctly 1970s flavour and an airy, open feel.

There was a rabbit warren of bedrooms, which remains in a way, but with hot and cold running water and all the quiet luxuries that you would expect from the generous owners: deep baths, giant showers, soft beds, feather-light eiderdowns and the comforting roar of the sea in the distance.

The house is largely single storey, but has many changes of level, buried into the hillside and emerging from it. Most rooms have wide French windows leading to the garden beyond, beautifully restored and reworked by the genius eye of Pip Morrison. This, after all, is really a house where you belong out of doors, tumbling through the jungle-like garden, down to the waves of the blue Cornish sea, deep in the bay below.

opposite In the basement of this handsome Arts and Crafts house, we restored a previously damp and decaying corridor. It has an austere simplicity, with white-painted walls, stone steps and a plain black-and-white vinyl sheet floor. The only preparation for the riches within is the oak door.

following pages Newly formed granite steps by Pip Morrison wrap around the old stone façade of the house, with mullioned, leaded-light windows into the hall. Erigeron daisies spill out everywhere. The view down to the wooded valley, and to the sparkling sea beyond, offers a glimpse of the *Scillonian* as she makes her way to the Isles of Scilly. The old house, with its many accretions, is the result of numerous phases of development over several decades. We restored the roof and renewed all the doors and windows.

Butterfly
Europa 25
Europa 25

opposite and above The Arts and Crafts entrance hall, with granite detailing and original doors. We sourced the Benson chandelier and painted the walls in 'Arsenic' from Farrow & Ball. Although once furnished as a sitting room, it very soon became much livelier with the arrival of a ping-pong table. The oak-framed doors, with their original hardware and hinges, were beautifully constructed and needed just a light-touch restoration after one hundred years.

right We created this new family room from a series of claustrophobic formal reception rooms, opening them up to become a light and airy space at the heart of the house. At one end is the kitchen; in the middle, a huge dining table, large enough for the whole family and many guests; and at the far end a seating area around a new granite fireplace designed by the studio. We decided to give the room a fresh 1970s feeling, with simple pine trusses and white-gloss-painted ceiling boards. French doors lead to the terrace, with glorious views down to the sea.

following pages The double doors in the family room lead to this cosy drawing room, with walls in 'Setting Plaster' by Farrow & Ball and comfortable sofas around the fireplace. The sofa on the left is covered in the famous ticking from Howard & Sons. We made the deep window seat, facing the sea, with cushions large enough to lie down and snooze upon. The paintings are by Algernon Newton (above the fireplace) and David Inshaw (above the sofa). Inshaw was a founding member of the Brotherhood of Ruralists, a famous 1970s artists' collective that sought inspiration in a mystical, figurative, pre-modern vision, strongly influenced by the Pre-Raphaelites a century earlier. The blue hydrangeas are from the garden.

left The heavy, dark-stained oak library was painted white and turned into a guest bedroom. A Schumacher fabric and wallpaper are used here, and in the adjacent bathroom.

opposite Clockwise from top left: an original tiled bathroom from the 1920s was retained and restored; joyous 'Spiral Willow' by Adelphi Paper Hangings in the downstairs WC; one of my Morris & Co. 'Honeysuckle' papers from the Cornubia collection in a guest bathroom; and a chinoiserie paper by Schumacher in the old library bathroom and bedroom.

following pages Late afternoon sunshine catches the old cedar tree in the hidden valley, which leads down to the sea. New granite walls were designed by Morrison. The photographs show the garden in its first proper summer. In the extraordinary west Cornwall microclimate, the house will be surrounded by a jungle within a few short years.

Settled in an Old Landscape

HAMPSHIRE, 2010–

Amid the roar of suburban life that can encroach on so much of the countryside in the south of England, there remain pockets of the landscape with that quiet feeling we all love deep in our bones. This is a farm in a beautiful unspoilt valley that still has the autumnal air of old England.

We were brought to the project by my great friend and collaborator Kim Wilkie, the landscape architect, who himself lives not far from this site. Our task was to enlarge a handsome, plain, mid-nineteenth-century farmhouse with a later Victorian wing. Kim, in his usual way, instantly realised that the sadness of the place was that the old farmhouse, facing south, with views over wonderful ancient buildings and a magnificent timber-framed barn, was actually looking at a car park.

His solution was to turn the house around, and to build a new driveway and entrance front on its north side. Together we designed a long, low brick-and-flint entrance façade that is intended to feel a completely seamless part of the whole. I wanted to work in an 'undesigned' way that would depend purely on materials and proportion to feel right. Everything you see in the foreground – flint garden walls, brick-and-flint wing, sash windows, slate roof and chimney – is just a few years old. I hope it has that feeling of having been here forever – the sense that if you were walking down this lane for the first time in a while, you'd look once, look twice and think, 'How is it possible I hadn't noticed that nice farmhouse before?' And walk on. This is the architecture of background, not foreground: the 'good ordinary'.

It is a house that took its theme and detail from another building in an attractive village not far away where we'd designed a new estate dower house – a project that sadly, for various reasons, remains unbuilt. Not a long time after came this commission and it is interesting how apt one idea can be for a different place. More recently, we've returned to build a small pavilion in the garden, to commemorate an important anniversary – an evolving project, where Kim has also spent a decade creating a beautiful masterplan of simple agricultural quality, flowers and vegetables being concentrated in a large and marvellous new walled garden. The surrounding land is being restored regeneratively with low-intensity grazing by traditional longhorn cattle: vernacular architecture, landscape and ecology in perfect synergy with one another, a mission that Kim and I try to bring to as many places as possible. It is a harmonious and balanced approach that feels all the more relevant in the face of the siren call to rewild.

opposite Autumnal tones of Boston ivy against the old brick-and-flint wall of the house, with a bed of bearded irises below.

following pages The brick-and-flint wing, with sash windows and slate roof, is completely new, maybe five or six years old at the time this photograph was taken. When Kim arrived here, he determined that the house should be turned around so that the old south-facing farmhouse no longer had to look over a car park. We conceived a masterplan that reoriented the house, and the resulting new wing is now the entrance front. The brick-and-flint garden walls in the foreground are also new. Beyond, to the left, is the striking black corrugated roof of the ancient threshing barn in the farmyard. To the right is the brick gable of the Victorian wing.

above The complex of farmyard buildings, orchard and farmhouse. At bottom right is our new brick-and-flint pavilion, completed in 2022 to commemorate an anniversary.

opposite Beautifully laid, new flint and brick in lime mortar: an ageless building. Flint, which is a building stone found in chalk, always feels settled and old.

following pages The house and a glimpse of the garden pavilion, sitting gently in their wooded valley. Mist rises with the morning light. The whitewashed building with clay peg-tile roof was existing, but everything else in this photograph is new.

Farmhouse of Memories

TUSCANY, ITALY, 2000–

In the rolling hills some fifteen miles to the north of Siena – unpretentious, agricultural Chianti – is a house I've known for longer than any other save the Old Parsonage. If it is possible for materials, such as stone and brick, to be vessels of our memories, nowhere for me is this truer than here.

This is the childhood home of my friend Valentina Rice and her brother Sebastian, who grew up both here and in London. Valentina and I met, and became instantly inseparable, in New York, but unlike many friendships that come and go in life, this one is like a limpet on a rock: the best kind, built on foundations that we know will last a lifetime. I don't have specific memories of the first time I saw Valentina's house – I think it may have been in the year 2000 – because so many summers here have followed that they have all merged into one happy rhythm. Valentina is a reassuring person of habit, and every year we eat the same delicious meals, under the comforting roof of the old *barchessa*. We do the same shop in the local town where the shopkeepers haven't changed in twenty years. The only shift comes in the weather, one year swelteringly hot, the next troubled by rumbling summer storms, but even this variety merges into one continuum of memory. There are sparks of dates that we can place with certainty – 2008, the year that Bruco (the local *contrade*) last won the Palio dI Siena – but I would say that these days I've watched maybe fifteen Palios, so those too blur into one.

This is a house, therefore, of extended, seamless, happy memories, of an evolving tribe of Valentina's holiday friends, which has, I suppose, shifted somewhat over the decades of her many friendships, to which she attends with unchanging care and generosity.

It's also the least decorated building in the book, but I included it because I can't think of a single house where I've been pottering around, making little interventions here and there, for so long. The house, like many family homes, was waiting for a shift of generations to tackle some demanding issues such as the roof, and the reworking of bathrooms and the kitchen. We've done all this with Valentina's brilliant house manager, Leda. But most of what we did was edit and move things around. There was a spectacular day (this I do remember well) – with our friends Adam and Nathan – when we dragged every single piece of furniture, except for some beds and huge wardrobes, out of the house and back in again. Each piece was reintroduced to the house in a different position. We turned an empty hall, filled with boxes of junk, into the beautiful main sitting room. We dusted and sorted and reworked all the bedrooms. As time and funds allowed, we tackled kitchens and bathrooms. And slowly a place evolves and takes shape, and matures and softens – never dependent on money, solely on ideas – just like the friendships it has nurtured.

opposite The old stone staircase leads to what would have been the original front door of the farmhouse. Most Tuscan farms of the seventeenth and eighteenth centuries had stables for the animals on the ground floor, with residential areas on the floors above it. The wooden table was made by the much-missed Berto, who for many decades looked after this land and the olive groves below the house.

following pages Left, clockwise from top left: an upper-floor bedroom; two views of the main living room, with its capacious fireplace and brick floor; the ground-floor sitting room. Right: a corner of the hallway, with the staircase that was inserted in the 1970s to join the two floors, avoiding the inconvenience of going outside to ascend or descend the original exterior stone staircase.

left One of the simple bedrooms, with a pair of nineteenth-century Italian bedsteads bought from a local junk shop, and block-printed Indian bedspreads from Country & Eastern of Norwich. I photocopied woodblock views of Tuscan towns from a nineteenth-century book, and tea-stained them in the sun before framing them in a collection of old frames. The hanging paper lampshade is original 1970s Habitat and must never be changed!

following pages Left, top: evening sun on the upper loggia, at the head of the exterior stair. Left, bottom: the remarkable view over blue Tuscan hills at dusk. Right: suppertime in the *barchessa*, waiting for one of Valentina's delicious and generous bowls of pasta to be brought to the table. This is the scene of many long and happy conversations deep into the evening, under the stars, to the sound of cicadas singing away in the darkness.

Vernacular Additions

SOUTH-WESTERN ENGLAND, 2017

Our approach to this group of buildings was about doing everything we could do not to be noticed – if we succeeded, no one would know we had been there. It's another project in brick and flint in a gentle chalk setting (see 'Settled in an Old Landscape' on pages 298–305), where I worked with Kim Wilkie, and where our collective vision was to apply the lightest touch imaginable.

At the core of the project was a handsome, large, unpretentious late Victorian threshing barn – just one of the many model farmyard developments that were built all over England in the later decades of the nineteenth century. It was the first time really that the ancient ways of agricultural life, undisturbed and unchanged for centuries, met the harsh realities of new industrial methods.

Thomas Hardy wrote elegies for that disappearing way of life, as he watched in horror at the hurtling new railways and machinery driving deep into the landscape of the old Wessex that he loved. Now, at the distance of one hundred fifty years, how gentle these buildings seem by comparison to the hideous monstrosities of modern agricultural industrial production.

Our task was to bring this derelict building, and ranges of cart sheds and stores, back into use, as a guest lodge at the heart of an estate where an ambitious programme of landscape regeneration is underway. Kim and I quickly developed a sense that we would complete three sides of a farm courtyard with a fourth. The sketches for the long range of not-quite-two-storey brick-and-flint buildings were developed very swiftly. It takes much more time today to detail everything to perfection and to ensure nothing goes wrong due to potential misinterpretations by builders. Sadly, in our era of building, it is impossible to leave anything to chance; inevitably, chance will produce glaring errors.

Buildings were taken down and rebuilt exactly as before, but with foundations and strengthened timbers, and roofs were put back with a broken ridgeline, to avoid feeling too new. The courtyard was planted with a simple meadow and four gnarled apple trees replanted from elsewhere. Perimeter paths were laid with great care in knapped flint, Kim's signature touch. A wildflower meadow has been planted in the fields around, filled with bees, and Kim has created a wide and serene reflecting dew pond.

Most of what you see here is brand new, or newly reconstructed. Now we are finished, can you tell that we have been here? I hope not.

opposite The flint-and-brick walls of the original Victorian threshing barn were meticulously restored, and the old cast-iron windows carefully cleaned and reinstated. The roof was lifted, new insulation installed and a reclaimed slate roof laid. We designed the glazed English-oak doors within the existing brick arches; you can see straight through these to the new range of brick-and-flint buildings that complete the east side of the farmyard.

following pages Kim and I conceived a range of new buildings to complete an open side of the farmyard. These buildings, which provide additional guest accommodation, are humble in scale, with the upper-floor windows tucked beneath the low eaves, close to the floor. Kim planted a beautiful meadow in the yard, with an apple tree in each corner.

right The cart shed was completely rebuilt, but in a way that we hope no one would know it has been touched. Today, its walls are hung with old agricultural implements, and it provides a generous covered outdoor dining area for summer evenings. Kim designed a simple gridded floor of handmade bricks.

opposite The brick-and-flint walls of the new guest range, whose detailing is drawn carefully from the old Victorian buildings to make a seamless addition.

above To the north of the original threshing barn we built this new wing on the site of an earlier barn. The pitch of the roof was clearly visible as a shadow on the old walls; perhaps it had once been thatched, but we could see evidence of clay tile and so this wing was roofed in a handmade clay tile that will weather down over time. We placed windows entirely at random on the façade, exactly where they needed to be for interior use, giving this elevation a quiet sense of integrity. Kim planted a beautiful wildflower meadow in front of the barn, around the newly created dew pond.

Seaside Holiday

CORNWALL, 2018

I don't know if the sharp-eyed reader would guess that this is a guest house in the grounds of the fine Jacobean castle we looked at in a previous chapter. Maybe it is the light where Cornwall meets Devon, or the distinct view over the estuary, or something about what we did here that chimes?

opposite A detail of the elegantly turned arms of an original Morris & Co. 'Sussex' chair, in an ebonised finish and with the original rush seat.

This was the first phase of what was meant to be a much larger architectural project, which (as described in 'A Jacobean Castle Revived' on pages 224–37) was greatly curtailed by the new circumstances we found ourselves in during the strange and restless years of the Covid pandemic. I really do see that as a fortunate outcome. Not everything needs to be completely rebuilt to be right – a lesson it's good to remind ourselves of from time to time.

But here was a building that was far gone. It had been converted from a barn in the late 1960s, and almost everything about it was broken: roof, windows, heating, floors, electrics and plumbing. The house has a curious flow, with tiny tight corridors and little dark rooms, and not enough living accommodation for the number of bedrooms.

We added two glazed wings on the ground floor, one as an extension of the sitting room, the other as a children's den. We knocked down walls and remodelled the interior to form a generous enfilade of sitting rooms, dining room and kitchen. We faced walls with Cornish slates to protect against decades of damp penetration. It was a massive overhaul. Halfway through construction we discovered an enormous bat colony living in a cavity wall. Bizarrely, not a single bat had shown up in the previous ecology surveys. The project closed for a few months while we worked out what to do with this particularly rare species.

When, finally, it was time to put the interiors back, we developed with our lovely clients an earthy palette of terracotta and olive green, turquoise and sky blue that drew directly from the colours of nature around us, while our friends Julian and Isabel Bannerman planted a dreamy garden. We bought furniture that was interesting but robust. It should not matter if anything got broken – a good rule in life generally, I'd say.

The pièce de résistance is the gloss-painted white-and-blue kitchen that we designed and built, and which most people believe has been in the house forever. That's decoration just how I like it – timeless and with the ability, I hope, to put a little smile on your face every morning.

opposite The dining room, with a view to the sitting room and new garden room beyond. It is painted in 'The Long Room', an archive colour by Paint & Paper Library, which has a warm intensity to it by day and a glow by night. A dry-scraped painted housekeepers cupboard contains china and linen. Around the dining table is a group of ebonised 'Wishbone' chairs by Hans J. Wegner, which speak across the century to the pair of Morris & Co. chairs on either side of the cupboard. Above the cast-iron radiator is a light fitting designed by my former boss, Charles Morris, a design the studio uses often.

right The new garden room, with boarded-timber ceiling, windows all around and rush matting on the floor: a sunny eating and sitting room. It adjoins the old sitting room, with its new fireplace and a denim-coloured sofa.

following pages This is perhaps my favourite kitchen of any that I've designed. The studio's standard detailing is made interesting and special by the two-tone coloration in white and blue paints, inspired by Cornishware pottery. We wanted to make a room that felt as if it had always been there. We intended to reuse the original sink unit, but tragically we discovered it had ended up on the builder's skip, despite very clear instructions. A long search ensued to find a perfect replacement. The work top is blue Formica.

ECO
VER
ZERO

TARTINE BREAD

left Orange linen curtains in the principal bedroom, with wallpaper from Morris & Co., jute matting on the floor and a painted faux-bamboo chest of drawers bought from Drew Pritchard. The already eclectic mix is given further energy by the surreal painting by South African artist John Meyer. The flowers are from the garden.

opposite Walls in '4-050' from Papers and Paints, orange linen blinds and a bright red bathtub. The washstand is late Georgian. Sometimes you don't need more than this.

following pages Ancient oak trees frame the serene view down to the Lynher estuary at sunrise.

A Farm in Stone Country

OXFORDSHIRE, 2012

We are in the heart of the eastern Cotswolds, in the stone part of Oxfordshire, a beautiful and unspoilt landscape. On the edge of a village in the countryside to the north of Witney, we were asked many years ago to look at the remodelling and enlargement of a small Georgian farm.

It is not always easy to understand how to make things work, but here I felt great certainty. The old Georgian house, low ceilinged and with enormous charm, had an ugly Victorian gabled extension to the north. I wanted to turn the house around entirely, remodel the existing gable and build a new one opposite, and infill, to create a seven-bay house with a slightly earlier feel.

The council heritage officer had different ideas and a compromise beckoned. With hindsight, I wonder if these interventions are for the best; sometimes they are, but more often, not. You may judge for yourself whether you would prefer the house to have a two-storey central block, as I'd first designed it, or a single-storey linking wing on which the conservation department insisted – part of the 'negotiation with life' that I referred to in the Introduction. It's a strange world when bureaucracy collides with design, as I am sure many architects and designers reading this book may attest.

No matter – we planned the foundations to carry a wall and roof as I feel sure will one day happen here, when we're all dead and gone, or maybe even before. For now, my 'link' has tall arch-headed windows to give a sense of presence and scale.

The landscape and planting are by the talented Jinny Blom, who created the wonderful meadow. Jinny knows just when to start and to stop, something that not every garden maker understands. Angel Collins carried out the detailed planting. The building was executed for us by Christian Fleming, then just starting out, now making so many beautiful houses of his own.

To the side is my favourite part of the building, with the columned loggia that provides a nice area of shelter for bikes and life stuff at the back door; and then the long, low wing that forms the back of a pool house – a building I feel very happy with. The round bulge was the result of a last-minute request from the client for a pizza oven next door to the fireplace we had already designed. Sometimes the best things in life come by accident, and this is the best of them all.

opposite A simple stone surround with robust detailing to the arched ground-floor windows of our new central block of the house (seen in the oblique on page 336). The westering sun casts long shadows. The central block is just one room deep, with a distant view through to the south.

following pages The entirely new range of structures built to the west of the house to form a new swimming pool building. With its completely gentle, vernacular feel, on the garden side the building opens up with an arcade overlooking the swimming pool garden designed by Jinny Blom. The one small window lights a pool changing room, and the pizza oven, next to the open fire with its tall chimney, was a late but aesthetically fortuitous request from the clients.

opposite The back door (top) is approached via a stone open loggia, providing shelter and a home for bikes and logs. To the left is the existing gabled wing of the old house (bottom), which we doubled in size.

My original design had the central section as a two-storey element, but it was pushed down to a single storey by the council heritage officer – something I found curious at the time, and still do.

above The simplicity of Grange Hill stone, with Hartham Park dressings, and a reclaimed Cotswold stone roof. Light and shadow do all the real work.

following pages A wildflower meadow lines both sides of the new driveway, all the creation of Jinny Blom: an astonishing sight as the sun rose on an already hot July morning.

West Coast Story

MID-ARGYLL, SCOTLAND, 2018–

Home at last. This is our happiest place, where Charlie, the dogs and I always feel at our best. I can't quite describe it, but we know it as soon as we get there. Maybe it starts with sleep, because we all sleep the sleep of ages here.

Am I allowed to end a book called *An English Vision* in Scotland? I hope you will forgive me, and of course you will have noticed that there is a rhythm of wonderful Scottish projects dancing throughout these pages. But I am an Englishman, not Scots, so I hope an English person is still permitted a vision that belongs in Scotland too – not least because I am married to a New Zealander directly descended from two families who made that long and arduous journey from Islay and Mull, in the harsh 1860s, never again to return to their homeland. It is fitting, perhaps, that we've ended up in a landscape with a view to both islands, from where Charlie's family left 160 years ago.

People often ask, 'How did you find the bothies?', but the rather dull answer is just like everything else: they were advertised online by an estate agent. A sharp-eyed friend, who knows who he is, was helping us to find somewhere and alerted us to the sale. I moved fast and headed north, and knew at first sight they were what we'd been searching for over the last four years.

We did very little when we first moved in, just fixing the roof and putting in new windows and doors. That's all we had money for. We get our water in a bucket from a spring, and our loo is a composting toilet (a different bucket!). We have no central heating and no plumbing. But we do have some lovely chintz curtains and a strong line in Wemyss Ware.

There are two buildings (which you can also see on page 18): the slate-roofed cottage, which we think is late nineteenth century, and the much earlier bothy, I guess from the early eighteenth century (but who is to say) and which originally would have been heather or reed thatched, now reroofed in red corrugated iron. The former contains our bedroom and sitting room; the latter our kitchen, which really does feel like living in a historic museum, especially in an arctic winter.

As I write, our tectonic plates are shifting, as we have slowly, gently, developed our plans for the existing houses, and a new little cottage that we have started building now. When it is all done, we think we will make a permanent move north, like homing pigeons, coming back to our roost – home at last.

opposite In the Victorian cottage, we have this Aesthetic Movement glass-fronted cabinet, filled with a collection of antique coral and shells. The chintz is 'Camilla' by Jean Monro, which we made into curtains and slipcovers after washing it to soften the fibres. The chairs are old, with their original velvet fabric. On top of the cabinet is our growing collection of Wemyss Ware.

following pages The cottage, with its original matchboarded pine interior, is incredibly cosy on a chill winter's day. The sofa is slipcovered in the same Jean Monro chintz. We bought the oak bookcase from Ally von Westenholz, and the ottoman from Paul Farnham of Bridport. The paper geranium is from The Green Vase. The charts belonged to my dad, who had used them for many years for west coast sailing cruises – these are all local places.

SOUND OF ISLAY

GAVIN MAXWELL
SCRABBLE
THE LEAVES RETURN

above Clockwise from top left: a painted motif on our Aesthetic Movement cabinet; shells and Victorian corals; the beautiful Edwardian stitching on our ottoman, bought from Paul Farnham; and a small nineteenth-century mug against a contemporary slipware platter bought from my friend Phoebe Clive, who owns Tinsmiths in Ledbury.

opposite Our bedroom is also in the cottage. Here is a grouping of religious lusterware on the wall above a washstand designed by Augustus Pugin (we get our water from the spring in a bucket). Part of our collection of Victorian Staffordshire figures sits atop the fireplace mantel. The model ship was from Islington Antiques, and the wool sample box from Drew Pritchard. The patchwork bedspread was made by my mother.

Prepare to meet thy God
THOU GOD SEEST ME.
THOU GOD SEEST ME.
THOU GOD SEES'T ME
THOU GOD. SEES'T ME.
PREPARE, TO MEET THY GOD.

right In the tin-roofed bothy, currently just a tidied-up shell while we work out our next plans, we have created an austere but practical kitchen. An Orkney rush chair sits next to the fireplace. With a roaring fire in here we can just about get warm in the winter. Our tin bathtub is in the corner, which we fill with hot water and enjoy in front of the fire.

following pages A view of the bothy from up the hill, with a magical mist rising off the sea during a summer day's sunrise. The landscape around us is rich with wildlife and sea life – a wonderful place to be, on what feels like the edge of civilisation.

BREAD

ACKNOWLEDGEMENTS

My first thanks are to all those who have been our clients and collaborators over these last two decades, and especially to those who have so generously allowed me into their houses, with my camera, over the last three years, to take photographs for this book.

John Moray has been a client for nearly all this time, the visionary landowner at Tornagrain. It was so kind of him to agree to write the Foreword.

All of these projects are themselves a collaboration. First, there are the many people who bring their talents to the Pentreath Studio, in all its facets. We are a wonderful and richly talented group with a common purpose and a real sense of humour, which is often needed! Thank you for putting up with me when I've got too much on, for chasing me down the street when we're walking to the station, and for taking such care and attention with every task we do.

Nothing would happen without the talented builders, housing developers, engineers, other architects, craftspeople, furniture makers, antique dealers, upholstery specialists, carvers and artists with whom we work to bring our visions into reality. Building or making anything these days is not an isolated art: it never was, but now more than ever it relies on huge groups of people with a shared approach to doing things well.

Making time in life to stop and record our work is never easy. Thanks to my fellow directors – Jennifer Bell, Rupert Cunningham, Rob Illingworth and Tamara Lancaster – for so kindly covering my long absences, and for everything they do within the practice, and especially to Zoe Wightman for all she has done to help in so many ways. Bridie Hall, with whom I have run Pentreath & Hall for fifteen happy years, has been equally tolerant of my long absences into the world of writing and photography.

George Saumarez Smith read an early proof of the book and gave me his invaluable thoughts; Ruth Guilding did the same, patiently, with the final drafts. Veere Grenney provided some brilliant advice in the earliest days, and Flora Soames and Beata Heuman – also fellow Rizzoli authors – have been very kind with their thoughts more recently. Thanks also to Ben Bolgar of the Prince's Foundation for his help and advice. Valentina Rice is one of my oldest friends and knows everything about books (and has kindly tutored me on many occasions); she also has one of the most beautiful houses in this book. Valentina introduced me to my kind and wonderful agent, Zoë Pagnamenta.

Robert Dalrymple is the supreme graphic designer. I've known Robert for thirty years, since I was at Edinburgh University, and it was the best good fortune that he has worked on so many striking books for Rizzoli, so this was a natural fit. We worked together, for an intense week, at Robert and Anna's beautiful house at Broadwoodside, laying out each page as a team, in the middle of storms, power cuts, gorgeous autumnal days and generous suppers. It was one of the happiest creative weeks of my life.

Philip Reeser has been a wonderful, friendly, intelligent editor at Rizzoli, always patient despite the long delays brought on by the pandemic and my general office workload. Philip joined us at Broadwoodside and brought the final magic to the pages. His attention to detail thereafter has been beyond my furthest expectation. Thanks to all his colleagues at Rizzoli, especially Charles Miers, for bringing my vision to life.

Finally, to Charlie, who's been so unfailingly patient and kind with the many disruptions that the book has brought to our lives, including my middle-of-the-night departures to capture sunrise in Cornwall or long absences over many weeks to find an elusive sunset in Scotland.

THE RICHARD H. DRIEHAUS PRIZE
AT THE UNIVERSITY OF NOTRE DAME

In March 2023 I was awarded the Driehaus Prize, which is given each year to 'a living architect whose work embodies the highest ideals of traditional and classical architecture in contemporary society, and creates a positive cultural, environmental and artistic impact'. The prize, founded by Richard Driehaus (1942–2021), is very generous, and there is no doubt that it gave me some additional freedom this year to complete this long-overdue book. My greatest thanks are due to Richard, and especially to the University of Notre Dame.

opposite A classical urn catches the morning sun on the terrace of the Oxfordshire swimming pool building we designed in 2006 (see page 172). The landscape planting is by Pip Morrison.

following page A beautiful watercolour wash drawing by the talented Anton Grain. This drawing shows the cross section of an ideal villa, based on Mereworth Castle, which we designed for an imaginary site during the lockdown summer of 2020.

First published in the
United States of America in 2024 by
Rizzoli International Publications, Inc.
49 West 27th Street
New York, New York 10001
rizzoliusa.com

Publisher: Charles Miers
Senior Editor: Philip Reeser
Production Manager: Kaija Markoe
Copy Editor: Linda Schofield
Managing Editor: Lynn Scrabis

Designer: Robert Dalrymple

Text by Ben Pentreath
Foreword by the Earl of Moray

Front and back endpapers:
'Willow Bough' in olive and turquoise from the Queen Square collection, a collaboration between Morris & Co. and Ben Pentreath / Distributed by Sanderson Design Group

ISBN: 978-0-8478-6667-0
Library of Congress Control Number: 2023949615

2025 2026 2027 2028 / 10 9 8 7 6 5 4

Printed in China

The authorized representative in the EU for product safety and compliance is
Mondadori Libri S.p.A., via Gian Battista Vico 42, Milan, Italy, 20123
www.mondadori.it